A Captive Audience

A Captive Audience

A Captive Audience

Voices of Japanese American Youth in World War II Arkansas

Edited by
Ali Welky

BUTLER
CENTER
BOOKS

BUTLER
CENTER
BOOKS

The Butler Center for Arkansas Studies
Central Arkansas Library System
100 Rock Street
Little Rock, Arkansas 72201

www.butlercenter.org

First edition: October 2015

ISBN 978-1-935106-86-9
ISBN 978-1-935106-87-6 (e-book)

Manager: Rod Lorenzen
Book & cover design: Mike Keckhaver

Library of Congress Cataloging-in-Publication Data

A captive audience : voices of Japanese American youth in World War II Arkansas / edited by
Ali Welky. -- First edition.

pages: 118
Audience: Grades 7 and up
ISBN 978-1-935106-86-9 (pbk. : alk. paper) – ISBN 978-1-935106-87-6 (e-book) 1. World
War, 1939-1945--Arkansas--Youth–Juvenile literature. 2. Japanese Americans--Arkansas--
Biography--Juvenile literature. 3. World War, 1939-1945--Prisoners and prisons, American--
Juvenile literature. 4. Japanese Americans--Arkansas--Social conditions--20th century--Juvenile
literature. 5. Japanese Americans--Evacuation and relocation, 1942-1945--Juvenile literature.
I. Welky, Ali, editor of compilation. II. Title: Voices of Japanese American youth in World War II
Arkansas.

D769.8.A6C25 2015
940.53'1776785092535--dc23

2015028494

Butler Center Books, the publishing division of the Butler Center for Arkansas
Studies, was made possible by the generosity of Dora Johnson Ragsdale and
John G. Ragsdale Jr.

Arkansas
Humanities
Council

A Captive Audience is supported in part by a grant from the Arkansas Humanities Council
and the National Endowment for the Humanities.

Cover photo: Group of teenagers standing on top of a truck that is going
over a bridge. Kazuko "Kaz" (Tsubouchi) Fujishima and sister Takayo in
middle; Jerome, Arkansas, ca. 1942–1944. Courtesy of the UALR Center for
Arkansas History and Culture, Life Interrupted Collection

Cover artwork: (guard house) Sazuko Inouye—Rohwer Camp #59, 1942–
1945; watercolor on paper. Courtesy of the Butler Center for Arkansas
Studies, Rosalie Santine Gould–Mabel Jamison Vogel Collection

(barracks) Mas Kitake—Rohwer Camp #2, 1942–1945; watercolor on paper.
Courtesy of the Butler Center for Arkansas Studies, Rosalie Santine Gould–
Mabel Jamison Vogel Collection

Printed Library Materials, ANSI Z39.48-1984.

This is dedicated to each and every person whose youthful words are relayed in this book—your voices are still being heard.

"All I can do is live the days as they come, good and bad."
——Margaret Samejima, 1942, Rohwer Relocation Center

"I just thought I was leaving piles of gold back there, and if the war should end, I thought I would like to go to my hometown to see the piles of gold again."
——Emiko Taguchi, 1942,
Rohwer Relocation Center

Oh as I was young and easy in the mercy of his means,
Time held me green and dying
Though I sang in my chains like the sea.
——from "Fern Hill" by Dylan Thomas, 1945

Table of Contents

You live in sunny California. Your dad is a farmer, or maybe he's a shop owner or a fisherman. Your mom maybe works on the farm, too, and runs the household. You go to school with your friends. Some of them are Japanese American like you; some aren't. You like to draw, or maybe play sports or design clothes. You listen to the radio all the time. You're looking forward to Christmas, although you know better than to wish for snow. Your little brother annoys you. You're worried about an algebra test coming up. You play the flute, or maybe the French horn. You wonder if your partner in biology lab thinks you're cute or has noticed you at all. You think maybe you'd like to be a farmer when you grow up. Or maybe a doctor. A teacher. An engineer. A seamstress.

And then, on December 7, 1941, with bombs falling from the sky, everything changes. Japan has attacked America, bombing its naval base at Pearl Harbor in Hawaii. Twenty-four hundred people are dead, and America is now at war with Japan.

Japan.

Your father was born in Japan. Or maybe your mother was, or your grandmother. You are Japanese American, born in California. But maybe you've been to Japan, or to Hawaii, to visit relatives. Or maybe to attend school there for a few years. Maybe you attend Japanese school in America, to learn the language and traditions of your ancestors. But you're an American, just like your white friends. Right?

You return to school the next day, dazed like everyone else. How could America—the land of the free—be under attack? At war? And why is everyone looking at you strangely now? Surely they don't think that *you're* the enemy? Your heritage is Japanese, but you're an American!

Rumors start about Japanese Americans, who have been living and working on the West Coast for many years following an influx of Asian immigrants to America starting in the late 1800s. The West Coast is now seen as vulnerable to attack, and Japanese Americans are under suspicion for aiding the enemy. Fear, hysteria, and rumors increase. Newspapers and other media feed the frenzy of public suspicion of Japanese Americans—Send them away! Put them in jail! Ship them back to Japan!

Away? Back to Japan? But you live in California. You're going to graduate from high school soon. Aren't you?

But the rumors you've been hearing about the Japanese Americans being sent away turn out to be true. President Franklin D. Roosevelt issues Executive Order 9066 on February 19, 1942, designating "exclusion zones" from which people of Japanese ancestry would be evacuated, including the western parts of California, Oregon, and Washington, as well as southern Arizona.

Exclusion zones? How can you be excluded from where you live? But excluded you are. And if you can't live in California anymore, where *can* you live? The U.S. government sees to that, beginning the mandatory evacuation and relocation of Japanese Americans, starting in spring 1942.

First you go by train to the Santa Anita Racetrack, near Los Angeles. A *horse* track? You would live like a *horse*? You bring only what you can carry, just a suitcase. Maybe you bring your precious baseball cards, your diary. Your favorite book. What clothes will you need where you are going? It doesn't matter—you can't fit many in your suitcase anyway. You leave behind your radio, your records, your books. Your little brother brings his teddy bear. You try to be patient with him, even though he's crying and asking you questions you don't know how to answer. Your family leaves behind everything. Your mom tries to put things in storage, but who knows for how long? Who knows if your possessions will be there when you get back? Will you ever even *get* back? If you do, how will your friends treat you?

Rohwer Relocation Center in Arkansas.
Courtesy of the Butler Center for Arkansas Studies, Edna A. Miller Collection

You spend months at Santa Anita, housed in a horse stall with your family. It's hot. It's crowded. It's miserable. But it's temporary, they say. Soon you will move to a permanent relocation center, they say.

And then one day in early fall, you board a train to Arkansas.

Arkansas?

Where is Arkansas?

When you get there, your new life begins. Or is it just a break in the middle of your regular life? What is your regular life anyway? Will it ever be regular again?

All you can do is observe your new world, navigating it as best you can—part of a captive audience, trying to live your life inside a perimeter of barbed wire.

Walking in Their Shoes
The people who had to leave their homes to go to the camps could bring very few items with them—only what they could carry. If you had to leave your home today for an uncertain future, what would you bring? What could you fit in a suitcase? Books, photos, mementos, a journal, art supplies? Remember that, when these young people left their homes in 1942, there were no mp3 players, televisions, computers, or smartphones!

11

How can we see the internment experience first-hand through the eyes of these captive young people, more than seventy years later? How can we attempt to experience what they experienced and observe what they observed right along with them? How can we hear their voices, still strong across the decades? And a better question still: Why is it important that we try?

Many people of Japanese descent who were incarcerated during this time have looked back on their experiences in interviews or by writing memoirs, offering valuable insight into the turbulent times, especially after gaining some perspective on the experience. My purpose here, however, is to attempt to get inside the heads of the young people facing this disruption to their normal lives *in real time* to see their perspectives on what was happening in the country and in the world. The teenagers held in the camps—more than anyone else there, really—seem caught in the middle in many ways: between childhood and adulthood, between their Japanese heritage and their American citizenship, between their lives before the relocation and what they would make of their lives afterward.

Rohwer High School yearbook editor Shinya Honda, from Résumé Yearbook; 1944.
Courtesy of the Butler Center for Arkansas Studies, Rosalie Santine Gould–Mabel Jamison Vogel Collection

Fortunately, we have some artifacts from this time that capture these voices. Specifically, here in Arkansas, we have preserved in historical archives items from this time, including photographs, yearbooks, newsletters, and, maybe most significantly for my purposes here, about 200 autobiographies written by tenth and eleventh graders at Rohwer High School in 1942, as well as post-war plans written in 1944. These materials are a crucial part of the historical record of this time, and I am honored to be able to give them a wider audience. Researchers also have, thankfully, access to many secondary works of analysis to draw on to give historical context to the experiences of these young people. And all that has been published so far—including this book—barely scratches the surface of this important subject. This book is in no way intended to be a comprehensive history of this complex event.

The autobiographies excerpted in this book give a glimpse into the world of these young people, a world that had been turned upside down. When you read their words, a few things become apparent. First, most seem to have been living the life of a typical American teenager on the West Coast, going to school, hanging out with friends, and engaging in sports and other activities. They—and particularly their parents and grandparents—might have faced some prejudice for their Japanese heritage (it was certainly present even before the war), but not much is revealed about it. These young people probably had a fairly strict, traditional homelife with significant Japanese cultural influence, but most seem to have viewed themselves as Americans first and foremost. Second, they heartbreakingly reveal that relocation was a significant disruption to their lives—and an unexpected one. Quite a few declare it to be the worst thing that had ever happened to them. They are uncertain about what it will mean for their futures.

Finally, there is a clear sense of relief and positivity that comes through about their arrival in Arkansas. This seems puzzling at first—how can they be upbeat and relieved to be in a remote, swampy collection of barracks?—until you remember what they had gone through before arriving in Arkansas: fear and prejudice on the West Coast following the bombing of Pearl Harbor; uncertainty and waiting; temporary and filthy housing—mostly in horse stalls at the Santa Anita Assembly Center or in barracks at the Stockton Assembly Center; and then a long train ride to more permanent housing in Arkansas, in a part of the country most had never visited before.

In Arkansas, although conditions were far from ideal or even comfortable, some sense of normality returned. They were in school. They were beginning activities such as art and sports. They could renew and develop friendships with others who were in the same strange, leaky boat as they were.

By collecting some of the voices of these young people as they observe their surroundings and circumstances, I hope to offer today's readers a chance to hear these voices, too. And, along the way, I think it will become apparent why it is important to listen.

———Ali Welky, editor
2015

Editor's note:
Small errors and irregularities in spelling, punctuation, and syntax in the autobiographical writings used for this book have been silently corrected so as not to distract from the content. Occasionally, additional or clarifying information is provided in brackets. When text is left out, ellipses have been used. Excerpts from autobiographical writings appear with the writer's name in blue.

I have predominantly drawn from the following collections of material from the internment camps in Arkansas.

The Butler Center for Arkansas Studies at the Central Arkansas Library System in Little Rock holds an extensive collection of Rohwer materials preserved by Rohwer art teacher Mabel Rose Jamison "Jamie" Vogel and kept after her death by her friend Rosalie Gould. This collection contains documents, artwork, and photographs, as well as about 200 autobiographies written as a class assignment in 1942, and a number of post-war plans written in 1944. They can be accessed in full in the Research Room of the Arkansas Studies Institute building in Little Rock. The finding aid to the collection can be accessed on site or online.

Rosalie Santine Gould–Mabel Jamison Vogel Collection, BC.MSS.10.49, Butler Center for Arkansas Studies, Central Arkansas Library System, Little Rock, Arkansas.
   http://arstudies.contentdm.oclc.org/cdm/compoundobject/collection/findingaids/id/5113/rec/6

The Butler Center also holds the Edna A. Miller Collection, which includes materials pertaining to the Rohwer Relocation Center. The materials are the personal memorabilia of Edna A. Miller, who was senior clerk-stenographer for Rohwer Project Director Ray D. Johnston. Included are camp newspapers, yearbooks, photographs, and other miscellaneous documents. They can be accessed in full in the Research Room of the Arkansas Studies Institute building in Little Rock. The finding aid to the collection can be accessed on site or online.

Edna A. Miller Collection, MSS.02.05, Butler Center for Arkansas Studies, Central Arkansas Library System, Little Rock, Arkansas.
   http://arstudies.contentdm.oclc.org/cdm/compoundobject/collection/findingaids/id/6181/rec/9

Also available in the Research Room of the Arkansas Studies Institute building—which houses the Arkansas history collections of both the Butler Center and the University of Arkansas at Little Rock (UALR) Center for Arkansas History and Culture—is UALR's Life Interrupted Collection: The Japanese American Experience in WWII Arkansas. The collection contains documents, photographs, oral histories, and other materials. The finding aid to the collection can be accessed on site or online.

Life Interrupted Collection, 1903–2005, UALR.MS.0250. University of Arkansas at Little Rock (UALR) Center for Arkansas History and Culture, Little Rock, Arkansas.
   http://arstudies.contentdm.oclc.org/cdm/compoundobject/collection/findingaids/id/5137/rec/45

Acknowledgements

This book would not have been possible without the wealth of materials from the Rosalie Santine Gould–Mabel Jamison Vogel Collection, donated to the Butler Center for Arkansas Studies by Rosalie Gould in 2011. These documents, photographs, and works of art first found a home with Rohwer art teacher Jamie Vogel after the war, then with Rosalie Gould after Vogel's death, and then, finally, at the Butler Center. They were kept in Arkansas for students, researchers, and the public to learn from and enjoy for years to come. This donation also continues to inspire others to add to the Butler Center's collection of materials from the camps in Arkansas, furthering the mission of educating people about what happened in the past and how that affects the present and future.

Many people have helped with this project in myriad ways. I'd like to thank Shannon Lausch and Kimberly Wessels Kaczenski at the University of Arkansas at Little Rock for helping me find and access marvelous photos from UALR's Life Interrupted Collection. I also appreciate UALR's permission to reprint these photos in this book. The Arkansas History Commission, particularly Lauren Jarvis, also provided permission to use materials as well as access to photos. Susan Gallion at the WWII Japanese American Internment Museum in McGehee was very helpful in providing information. I'm also indebted to the scholarship of Russell Bearden and of Dr. Jan Ziegler, whose writings provided me with context and insight into internment in Arkansas, particularly the educational experience. Nancy Chikaraishi of Drury University in Springfield, Missouri, whose parents were interned at Rohwer, allowed me to use her powerful artwork, and her father, Ben Chikaraishi, generously gave his permission to share his writing.

I'd also like to thank a number of Butler Center colleagues. Steve Teske cheerfully helped me navigate the Butler Center's collection on numerous occasions. Brian Robertson provided materials, answers, and guidance, as did Nathania Sawyer, Michael Hodge, and Colin Thompson. Several others helped spur along the publication of this book, including David Stricklin, Bob Razer, Guy Lancaster, and, especially, Rod Lorenzen—who had the original idea for a book about internment in Arkansas. Rod also typed his fingers to the bone transcribing autobiographies for me. I would also like to express my appreciation to Kay Bland for all her efforts over the years to bring historical resources to young people in Arkansas. And I can never thank Mike Keckhaver enough for his beautiful design work on the cover and pages of this book.

And thanks to my family, including my very favorite historian, for everything and then some.

As one of its many good works, the Arkansas Humanities Council provided a publication grant for this book, for which I am very grateful.

Finally, I'd like to thank all the people whose voices, images, and artwork are found in this book. Their honesty and courage during these tumultuous times are an inspiration. I'm also indebted to those who preserved materials from the relocation centers—Jamie Vogel, Rosalie Gould, Edna Miller, and many others—allowing us to learn from them indefinitely.

Arkansas's Relocation Centers[1]

During World War II, thousands of people—based on their ethnic heritage alone—were rounded up, assigned family numbers, and moved into camps where they lived in barracks surrounded by barbed wire and guard towers. Two of these camps were in Arkansas. This happened right here, in the United States of America.

Aerial view of Rohwer Relocation Center.
Courtesy of the UALR Center for Arkansas History and Culture, Life Interrupted Collection

After the Japanese Empire's attack on Pearl Harbor on December 7, 1941, U.S. military leaders thought that the large number of Japanese Americans living on the West Coast presented a threat to national security. On the advice of military leaders who feared collaboration between Japan and Japanese Americans, President Franklin D. Roosevelt issued Executive Order 9066. This order gave the secretary of war the power to designate military areas from which "any or all persons may be excluded" and authorized military commanders to initiate orders they deemed advisable to enforce such action.

World War II had a great impact on the lives of Americans. But no group was affected more than the 120,000 people of Japanese descent living in America, mostly on the West Coast. The federal government forcibly rounded up these Japanese Americans and sent them by train to what were, in the president's own words at the time, "concentration camps." The Japanese Americans were given very little time to settle their affairs, sell or store their property, and report to the evacuation centers. Notices were posted in the Japanese American communities instructing them to bring only what they could carry—including bedding, dishes, utensils, clothing, and personal items.

Map of Internment Camps. *Map created by Mike Keckhaver*

Eventually, ten camps were established—all located in remote areas with sparse populations and no potential military targets. Arkansas was home to two of these so-called relocation centers: one at Jerome and one at Rohwer. Approximately sixty-four percent of the Japanese Americans who were relocated were American citizens. Nearly 17,000 people came to the state in the largest influx of any ethnic group in Arkansas's history.

Why Arkansas? Swaths of its publicly owned land met the War Relocation Authority (WRA) criteria of offering work opportunities for evacuees (such as clearing land); good conditions for growing food, such as soil, water supply, and growing climate; and adequate transportation, such as roads and train routes.

Arkansans were not generally welcoming to the Japanese Americans in their state. Local residents were often hostile to those imprisoned in the camps for reasons beyond the race of the internees. The camps often had amenities that were lacking in the poor, Delta towns that surrounded them: electricity, plentiful food, and more. During the period of confinement, many unfounded and malicious accusations of "coddling," food hoarding, labor strikes, and disloyalty were aimed at the camps and their residents by state political leaders.

Arkansas governor Homer Adkins and others also resented and feared the Japanese American prisoners. On February 13, 1943, the Arkansas state legislature passed the Alien Land Act "to prohibit any Japanese, citizen or alien, from purchasing or owning land in Arkansas." This

Terminology of Confinement

There is much debate about how to refer to both the Japanese Americans involved and the facilities themselves. At the time, the people held were usually called **evacuees**, but many historians say that terms such as **detainee**, **inmate**, or **prisoner** are more accurate. The facilities were often called **relocation centers** or **internment camps** at the time, but some people think they should be called **prison camps** or **concentration camps**. The term **concentration camp** is a problem, however, because of the association with Nazi death camps during World War II.

This book will use terms somewhat interchangeably, often based on the words of the Japanese Americans themselves, but one fact remains: the people held in the centers were not merely "relocated" or "evacuated"—they were imprisoned under armed guard.

Somewhat confusingly, the term **relocation** can refer to both the first roundup and detainment of those of Japanese ancestry as well as their later movement out of the camps during or after the war to new homes; however, the term **resettlement** is often used for post-war situations.

(For more information, see the Civil Liberties Public Education Fund Resolution Regarding Terminology at http://www.momomedia.com/CLPEF/backgrnd.html#Link to terminology.)

Communal bathhouse, laundry facilities, and mess hall at Rohwer.
Courtesy of the Butler Center for Arkansas Studies, Edna A. Miller Collection

act was later ruled unconstitutional, and after the camps closed, several families remained in Arkansas. All but one (that of Sam Yada) left within a year's time.

Governor Adkins was particularly opposed to letting Japanese Americans attend college within the state, fearing that allowing such would pave the way to the integration of higher education in Arkansas; at this time, black and white students did not attend school together.

Though most in the state had little use for them, some Japanese Americans found that the federal government had plans for them. Around the same time that Arkansas's government passed the Alien Land Act, the U.S. Army initiated a forced loyalty and draft program targeting Japanese American prisoners; this program pulled 326 youth from the Rohwer and Jerome camps. Those of age for military service were often conflicted when it came to the possibility of serving. Some were eager for the opportunity to prove themselves to the country of their birth, while others were resentful of being asked to sacrifice their time, and possibly their lives, on behalf of the country that had imprisoned them without cause.

The internment experience devastated and fragmented many Japanese American families. Fathers saw their role as breadwinners usurped by an American police state. Mothers attempted to maintain their roles as keepers of domestic comfort and harmony in these trying circumstances. Families struggled to find privacy and dignity in cramped, single-room quarters, with walls that did not extend to the ceiling. Many camps experienced outbreaks of diseases such as malaria, dysentery, typhoid, and tuberculosis. Camp schools faced a shortage of teachers and educational supplies.

Despite local residents' reluctance to embrace the Japanese Americans, stores and other businesses in the towns around the Rohwer camp, for instance, benefited from the increased expenditures in the area. Too, the Japanese Americans worked

Local businesses bought space in the 1944 Rohwer High School yearbook to advertise to the camp residents.
Courtesy of the Butler Center for Arkansas Studies, Rosalie Santine Gould–Mabel Jamison Vogel Collection

Generational Terms Used by Japanese Americans

Children who were born in America to Japanese parents were American citizens, but it was not until 1952 that Japanese and other Asian immigrants to the United States could become naturalized citizens. **Naturalization** is the manner in which a person not born in the United States voluntarily becomes a U.S. citizen. The term **alien** refers to a non-citizen who is allowed to remain in a country.

Issei
Born in Japan, first-generation immigrants who were denied U.S. citizenship

Nisei
The children of the Issei, born in America, U.S. citizens by birth and educated in the U.S., second-generation Japanese Americans

Kibei
The children of the Issei, born in America but educated in Japan

Sansei
The children of the Nisei (and grandchildren of the Issei), third-generation Japanese Americans

Yonsei
Fourth-generation Japanese Americans

to clear and drain the land upon which the camps were based; after the camps were closed, the land was auctioned off to local farmers for a low price.

At first, camp life offered little comfort. Parts of the facilities were still under construction, and they had few amenities. The camps quickly became small towns, however, with internal committees and organizations. Most of the residents worked at various jobs in the camps, which gave them some income, and the administration encouraged activities for their leisure time. The residents took classes in everything from judo to painting. Classes were taught by teachers brought in from the surrounding area as well as Japanese American internees who had skills in certain areas.

Rohwer Relocation Center[2]

The first Arkansas camp in operation, the Rohwer Relocation Center located on more than 10,000 acres in Desha County, officially opened in September 1942, although construction on it was not yet complete. Nearly 8,500 people were detained at the Rohwer camp from 1942 to 1945.

Families lived in cramped spaces in communal barracks. They stood in line for everything—to eat at lines of tables in the mess hall, to use latrines with rows of toilets sitting in the open, and to wash their clothes in large sinks at the laundry.

Rohwer was the last of all the internment camps in the nation to close (except for the higher-security segregation center at Tule Lake, which closed in March 1946). It ceased its operations on November 30, 1945—more than three months after the end of World War II. The WRA had a difficult time relocating Japanese Americans back to their old homes and jobs in California, and many families lost all their possessions during their imprisonment.

The buildings of the former Rohwer camp were used for local schools and by farmers for a variety of purposes before falling into ruin. The Rohwer National Historic Landmark, added

Japanese Americans in the U.S. Military

In 1941, the U.S. armed forces included more than 5,000 Japanese American soldiers. After the attack on Pearl Harbor, the military discharged many of these soldiers and classified civilians of draft age as "enemy aliens," despite their status as U.S. citizens.

In 1943, however, the War Department created the 442nd Regimental Combat Team, which was composed entirely of Japanese American soldiers. Many of the residents of the ten detention camps joined the 442nd, which became the most decorated unit of its size and duration in U.S. military history. These soldiers received more than 18,000 individual decorations for bravery, 9,500 Purple Hearts, and seven Presidential Distinguished Unit citations.

An art class draws portraits of a model in the recreation hall at Rohwer.
Courtesy of the UALR Center for Arkansas History and Culture, Life Interrupted Collection

to the National Register of Historic Places on July 30, 1974, contains several monuments made by inmates during their internment, including one in honor of Japanese American soldiers who died in World War II; a small cemetery; and the remnants of the hospital smoke stack.

Jerome Relocation Center[3]

The Japanese American incarceration camp at Jerome (in Drew County and partially in Chicot County) held nearly 8,500 at its peak: Japanese Americans from Los Angeles, Fresno, and Sacramento, California, as well as from Honolulu, Hawaii. The Jerome Relocation Center was in operation for 634 days (October 6, 1942, to June 30, 1944)—the fewest number of days of any of the ten relocation camps.

The Jerome site (officially designated as "Denson" by the post office) consisted of tax-delinquent lands in the marshy Delta of the Mississippi River's flood plain. The lands were in dire need of clearing, development, and drainage. The camp was built eight miles south of the small farming town of Dermott in Chicot County and was connected by rail to the Rohwer Relocation Center in Desha County by the Missouri Pacific Railway system. The entire Jerome site encompassed 10,054 acres between the Big and Crooked Bayous.

The compound eventually became nearly 500 acres of tarpapered, A-framed buildings arranged into numbered blocks. Each block was designed to accommodate around 300 people in fourteen residential barracks, with each barrack (20' x 120') divided into four to six apartments. (This was the traditional military style for barracks, though the internees rebuilt or remodeled the insides.)

Each block also included a recreational building, a mess hall, a laundry building, and a building for a communal latrine. All the residential buildings were without plumbing or running water and were heated during the winter months by wood stoves. The camp also had an administrative section that was segregated from the rest of the camp to handle camp operations, a military police section, a hospital section, a warehouse and factory section, a segregated residential section of barracks for white WRA personnel only, barracks for schools,

Rohwer by the Numbers

■ Over 90% percent of the adult Rohwer population of 8,475 had been involved in agriculture, commercial fishing, or businesses that centered on the distribution of agricultural products.

■ 53% of Rohwer's internees had formerly lived in rural communities, 42% had lived in towns of more than 2,500, and 5% had lived in towns of fewer than 2,500.

■ Just over half of the people at Rohwer came from the Santa Anita Assembly Center, while most of the rest came from Stockton.

■ 35% of the camp's population were Issei, 10% over the age of sixty.

■ 64% were Nisei, 40% under the age of nineteen.

■ 57% of the Rohwer population spoke both English and Japanese, 32% spoke Japanese only, and 7% spoke English only (the remaining population was too young to speak a language).

■ There were 2,447 school-age children at Rohwer—28% of the total population.

Elaine Simpson teaches a high school class at Rohwer; note the makeshift teacher's desk made from a crate.
Courtesy of the UALR Center for Arkansas History and Culture, Life Interrupted Collection

and other buildings used as canteens, movie theaters, gymnasiums, auditoriums, and fire stations.

Like Rohwer, the camp itself was partially surrounded by barbed wire or heavily wooded areas with guard towers situated at strategic areas and guarded by soldiers.

The incarcerated Japanese American youth at the Jerome camp had the most negative reaction to the army's forced loyalty and military draft program initiated in February 1943. Several hundred young Nisei peacefully marched to the camp director's building and petitioned against the program.

The first of the ten relocation camps to close (people remaining at Jerome moved mostly to Rohwer and to Gila River in Arizona), Jerome was used as a German prisoner-of-war camp until the end of the war in Europe.

> ### Jerome by the Numbers
> ■ In February 1943, the camp reached its maximum population of 8,497.
> ■ Most internees had been engaged in agricultural work before the war.
> ■ 33% of the men and women in Jerome were aliens (non-citizens)—14% over the age of sixty.
> ■ 66% percent were American citizens—39% under the age of nineteen.
> ■ There were 2,483 school-age children at Jerome—31% of the total population.

Today, the site is mostly used as farmland, although a monument marks the former camp. The WWII Japanese Internment Museum, which commemorates the internment experience at both Jerome and Rohwer, opened in McGehee in Desha County in 2013.

Guard tower at Rohwer.
Courtesy of the Butler Center for Arkansas Studies, Edna A. Miller Collection

Notes

1. Source for camps overview: Russell Bearden, "Japanese American Relocation Camps," Encyclopedia of Arkansas History & Culture, http://www. encyclopediaofarkansas.net/encyclopedia/ entry-detail.aspx?entryID=2273.

2. Sources for Rohwer overview: Densho Encyclopedia, "Rohwer," http://encyclopedia.densho.org/ Rohwer/; Russell Bearden, "Rohwer Relocation Center," Encyclopedia of Arkansas History & Culture, http://www. encyclopediaofarkansas.net/encyclopedia/entry-detail.aspx?entryID=369; and Jan Fielder Ziegler, *The Schooling of Japanese American Children at Relocation Centers During World War II: Miss Mabel Jamison and Her Teaching of Art at Rohwer, Arkansas* (Lewiston, NY: The Mellen Press, 2005), 160–61.

3. Sources for Jerome overview: Densho Encyclopedia, "Jerome," http:// encyclopedia.densho.org/Jerome/; Russell Bearden, "Jerome Relocation Center," Encyclopedia of Arkansas History & Culture, http://www.encyclopediaofarkansas. net/encyclopedia/entry-detail.aspx?entryID=2399.

Chapter 1
Voices: Pearl Harbor, Assembly Centers, and Leaving the West Coast for Arkansas

World War II had been raging in Europe since September 1939, with Germany invading Poland, and Britain and France then declaring war on Germany. In the Pacific, the Empire of Japan had been at war with Republic of China since 1937. Germany had formed the Axis alliance with Japan and Italy, and—in June 1941—Germany invaded the Soviet Union. In December 1941, Japan attacked U.S. and European territories in the Pacific Ocean, including a surprise attack on the U.S. naval base at Pearl Harbor, in what was then the U.S. territory of Hawaii. The United States declared war on Japan following the attack, joining the Allied powers of Britain, Russia, China, and others against the Axis powers. Germany and Italy then declared war on the United States. The war had truly become a world war.

Fear gripped the country in wartime, and that fear—coupled with longstanding prejudice against Japanese immigrants in America—became directed at Japanese Americans living on the West Coast. People thought they might sabotage U.S. military installations or spy for Japan.

The circumstances under which the teenagers held in the Rohwer camp left the West Coast and finally arrived in Arkansas were still very much on their minds as they wrote their autobiographies in November and December 1942 as a class assignment. They discuss their surprise and sadness at the bombing of Pearl Harbor and the beginning of the war; what it was like to leave behind their former lives, homes, schools, and friends; their temporary housing in California at the makeshift assembly center at the Santa Anita racetrack or at the Stockton Assembly Center; their journey to Arkansas by train; and their new life at Rohwer. Their stories exhibit sadness at what they left behind, sometimes anger, a resigned kind of relief at being settled at last in Arkansas for the duration of the war, and a sense of hope for the future.

But on December 7, 1941—"a date which will live in infamy," as President Franklin D. Roosevelt declared—Arkansas was the farthest thing from the minds of these California kids. The young people wrote in their autobiographies of their own shock and fear after Japan's attack on America, which brought the United States into World War II. A few months later, they and their families were sent to temporary assembly centers in California in advance of more permanent relocation to centers such as Rohwer and Jerome in Arkansas.

Mary Kobayashi
"Remember Pearl Harbor." I could still clearly remember that sunny December afternoon when I heard Hawaii, Pearl Harbor, had been attacked. Right there and then the world seemed to crumble from under my feet. My first thought was, what will the people think or feel towards us at school tomorrow? All day long I moped around the house with a face longer than a horse's. But, the incident that knocked the wind

out of me was when the man my father was working for was taken by the F.B.I. because they said he was an enemy alien and was very dangerous to this country.

The morning after at school, I am proud to say that everyone treated us like Americans, which we are, and believe me when I say that with the unity this country has we'll win this war!

The days that followed were hectic ones, with rumors flying thick. It became so that you could not believe anyone. Then came the curfew, which bonded us in our homes from eight at night to six in the morning. Banks closed their doors on us with our money, making us feel very insecure. Although all this was happening, the Caucasian teachers and my friends aided us in every way possible. I and many others helped in selling war bonds after school.

Again rumors came that General DeWitt [John L. DeWitt, U.S. Army general who recommended and then organized the relocation of people of Japanese descent] was evacuating all Japanese, both citizens and aliens alike, out of the strategic military zones and Terminal Island. This, of course, came true, and the papers had nothing but the evacuation news in them. All was quiet for a few months when, one day in April after Easter vacation, our neighbor came bursting in the house, yelling that we would be evacuated in a week. I didn't believe a word he said. But, a few days later, bulletins were put up all over the town informing all Japanese that we would soon have to leave. It seemed just like yesterday as I recall the rushing and storing of our household goods.

Japanese American boys in San Francisco, California, one with "Remember Pearl Harbor" emblazoned on his hat, await the bus to an assembly center; 1942.
Courtesy of Library of Congress Prints and Photographs Division

Thursday, April the ninth, was my last day in school. Saying goodbye to all my teachers and friends was very hard and sad. Everyone was kind and the members of the homeroom gave me a school pin to remember them by, while my gang gave me a going-away present. I received notes that day from my crowd telling me to keep my chin up and hope for the best, for we'll meet again some day.

Frank Sakioka

I went to Japanese school, which was like a church to me, all my life until the Pearl Harbor attack, Dec. 7, 1941, on Sunday, when we all had to quit Japanese school. I kept on thinking that it couldn't be true, but I remember the following day when the newspaper headline said, "Japs Open War With Bombing of Hawaii."

About a month later, we were "frozen" so that we couldn't go more than five miles from home. Then, came the evacuation notice. It kept me wondering why we, the American citizens, had to evacuate, for our record was as clean as it can be. And, it got me worried how the camp life was going to be.

Edna Ito

[After the evacuation order], Father and Mother stayed up late at nights to pack. Father had to sell all the stock in the grocery store in a few days, in order to rent the store to someone else. I dreaded most leaving our newly built house. Especially when I had to leave my new bedroom set my father bought for me, and where I only slept a few weeks. The night before entering the camps, I lay there in my bed thinking that I would not come back to this house until the war is over or maybe we won't be able to come home at all. I had a lump in my throat, and my eyes became wet. I am wishing and hoping that we could go back to our home and live a happy and normal life again, soon.

Midori Oura

What I enjoyed the most [back in California] were our impromptu picnics. If it promised to be a glorious day, and if we were in the right mood, someone was sure to say, "Let's go to the beach today!" If everyone agreed, we hustled up a little lunch—nothing special—bundled ourselves into the car and responded to the call of the sea in summertime. More than often, instead of going down to the sandy beach, we selected a grassy knoll beneath some trees, or frequently, beneath just the blue skies. We always came back tired, but rested, and happy. Since December 7, 1941, war had darkened our horizons.

Tom Saito

Well, I was just getting on to life and the best part of it when all this happened on December 7 of 1941. That day I did not go to church because I had a cold and I stayed home.

When I first heard the radio I didn't believe that the war had started but, as you know today, the war is a year old already. I can look back on that day and still remember all kinds of things going on but I hate to write about it.

About a month or two after Pearl Harbor, the F.B.I. came and took my father to a camp in Santa Fe, New Mexico.

Months later, when we got in camp at Santa Anita, he came back to us.

After he was taken away to the camp, we sold most things and some of them were stored for us at the church we attended. Then, after that, my mother, two sisters, Grandfather, Grandmother, and I went to live at my uncle's place in Los Angeles.

Mary Takemoto

The most recent and most important thing that has happened to me are the events that occurred since the day of December 7, 1941. On Monday, December 8th, I went to school feeling smaller than a "1-cent piece" for I thought people would point me out as a "Jap." Of course, some pupils did point us out but the majority, as a rule, were nice. It was indeed a day of emotional strain for me. School wasn't so bad to go to, but outside of school was quite terrifying, so therefore I ceased going to town so often and I discontinued going to weekly movies. I didn't care about the grades in school, and I didn't seem to care much for anything.

Nancy Suzuki

The experience of evacuation was my most exciting incident in my life. When I first heard the news that all the Japanese would have to evacuate, it was very shocking. At first, we thought we better move on our own accord to an unrestricted area. Before we had a chance, the new order came out that it couldn't be done, so we had to stay until being evacuated to the Assembly Center.

The thing that shocked all the Japanese American citizens

Little Tokyo in Los Angeles

At the beginning of the war in 1941, Little Tokyo, a predominately Japanese and Japanese American area of Los Angeles, had about 30,000 residents. Once the federal government excluded Japanese Americans from the West Coast in early 1942, the "Japantowns" up and down the West Coast were left empty. As Japanese immigrants by law had not been allowed to own property, the white owners of buildings and businesses where the Japanese residents had lived and worked had to find new tenants. African Americans, mainly from the South, started coming to California to fill defense-industry positions. For many African Americans, empty Japantowns like Little Tokyo became their home, as housing restrictions at the time barred black residents from white neighborhoods. The neighborhood was then dubbed Bronzeville.

Near the end of the war, the government began allowing Japanese Americans to return to the West Coast. These Japanese Americans began reopening businesses in Little Tokyo, and African Americans—whose defense jobs were ending as well—began moving out.

In 1992, the Japanese American National Museum opened in the Little Tokyo area.

(Source: Densho Encyclopedia, "Little Tokyo / Bronzeville, Los Angeles, California")

like me was the curfew hours from 8 a.m. to 9 p.m. It meant that we couldn't stay out later than 9 p.m. or go out before 8 a.m. We had our rights as American citizens but since it was enforced on us, we all obeyed the orders.

The evacuation took place early in May, 1941. During that time I was still attending school but was asked to quit school in order to help at home. I quit school quite early, leaving all my studies, which made it very bad for my grades.

While many of the young people in the Arkansas camps had lived in areas of the West Coast with a diverse population (including many whites and people of other races), some had lived in Japanese enclaves in California where they attended Japanese schools and were surrounded almost entirely with other people of Japanese heritage, including Little Tokyo and the fishing community of Terminal Island.

Chiyeko Narasaki

As we lived right in the middle of Lil Tokio [Little Tokyo, in Los Angeles] the effect of the sudden change was felt in our souls. F.B.I. walked into every building, searching and tearing pictures and images of Buddha from the walls. Japanese people lived in fear day and night. They burned every book, picture, photograph, images of Buddhists and Shintos.... Stores after stores were closed down by F.B.I. agents. The busy Lil Tokio town has changed in one day to a dead city. Who would have dreamed that today would bring suffering and unhappiness to us Japanese Americans?

Shiunro Hayashi

I was born on Jan. 1, 1926 on Terminal Island, California... located in the middle of Los Angeles Harbor. This island is about three and a half miles long and is surrounded by a channel. People have to ride on ferry boats or go across the bridge to get on the mainland. On one corner of this island is a Japanese Colony or otherwise known as Fish Harbor. About two to three thousand Japanese live here, together. The boys and girls speak Japanese at home as well as at school. They speak poor English. The Japanese here make their living by fishing and working at the fish canneries. [In camp,] we can buy canned fishes that have been canned in Terminal Island, at the Canteen. My father is a fisherman. He was away from home most of the time. My mother worked at the fish canneries....On the morning of December 7 we were all very surprised by the bombing of Pearl Harbor. That day many United States army soldiers came to Terminal Island. They had guns with bayonets fixed on the end and were patrolling every street in Terminal Island. About a month after the war started every alien Japanese fisherman was rounded up and put in concentration camps [detention camps where people were held for questioning]. We went to school normally every day until Feb. 26; an army order came that we had to move out of Terminal Island in forty-eight hours. Most of us did not have any place to go. Our family and a couple of other families moved to a Japanese school in Norwalk. Many of the other Terminal Islanders moved to Los Angeles....[They] all were moved to Manzanar Relocation Center.

Marian Yamamoto

Then came the fateful December 7th, war. At that time it seemed unbelievable. My country was fighting with Japan, the homeland of my parents. Many Japanese students then quit school, but I still kept on going to school.

One day, a notice to all Japanese citizens or non-citizens said we were to evacuate from Terminal Island within forty-eight hours. Then, I had to quit school and that hit me harder and had more effect upon me than anything in my life. Father was taken away by the F.B.I. We lost money and left most of our furniture laying down on the floor.

We then moved to Los Angeles to our friend's hotel. Never did I feel so lonely and stunned from such unpleasant news. How I hated to part with my friends and relatives.

At Los Angeles, I spent two months at the hotel. While staying there, I attended Belmont High School and some of my friends went there, too. From that day on, step by step, plans and orders were made which affected us until, at last, it led us into evacuation of all Japanese, citizen or non-citizen, and into relocation camps and assembly centers.

What Happened if You Didn't Leave?

Twenty-two-year-old Fred Korematsu found out. On May 9, 1942, his parents and three brothers reported to an assembly center, but Korematsu stayed with his Italian-American girlfriend instead, disguising his racial identity and taking a different name. He also underwent minor plastic surgery on his eyes to appear European American. His noncompliance with the evacuation order led to his arrest on May 30, 1942, and his eventual internment at the Topaz camp in Utah. He challenged the constitutionality of the government's wartime removal and confinement of Japanese Americans in what became the landmark Supreme Court case *Korematsu v. the United States*. The Court sided with the government against Korematsu, but it ruled in the case of *Endo v. the United States* (with the decision announced the same day as its *Korematsu* decision, December 18, 1944) that the government could not detain law-abiding citizens, thereby opening the door for Japanese Americans to begin returning to the West Coast. Korematsu was given a Presidential Medal of Freedom for his civil rights work in 1999. He died in 2005.

(Source: Densho Encyclopedia, *"Korematsu v. United States"*)

Margaret Samejima

Evacuation is one incident I will never forget. I will never forget how slowly our home became nothing. The way our furnishings were sold at such a very cheap price.

Nellie Utsumi

When war broke out on December 7, 1941, the minds of all the people were troubled, especially those of ours. At school it seemed as though everyone was talking behind our backs. At home Mother and Father had a worried look; not worried about themselves but about us. What is going to happen to us? Then the curfew law was passed. We were not able to go out after nine o'clock. It wasn't so bad then but the time was later changed to eight o'clock. At home we all sat around together and discussed the war situation. Finally, we heard rumors of being evacuated. Hurriedly, we sold our beloved store and started packing.

Nagako Horiguchi

When the war broke out in the year of 1941, I read in the paper three or four months later that the Japanese people living near the Pacific Coast must be evacuated. When I heard this, I didn't like it because it meant that I had to leave school, my friends from school, and the house I had lived in for 14 years in the same place.

About one month later we got our notice that it was our turn to evacuate. I went to school the next day and quit. I dropped school because I couldn't think or study. My mind was on us being evacuated and how we might be sent to some far place where we wouldn't be near the coast. My mother and father were also worried about this situation and didn't like quitting the farm business. But, I thought it was best to do so. My father had to quit the farm. The next day, he got a notice to come to register to Lawndale to get information about evacuating. When he went there, they took his name and asked him how many members there were in our family. They gave him a tag with the family number on it to be put on each person so they'll know who you are when you're being evacuated. Also, they told him the things which he should not take with him. They told him he could only take suitcases and a little of your belongings etc., just so you don't have much. When he came home and told us about it, we knew we didn't have enough suitcases to pack our clothes. My father took the furniture, dishes, books, and many other things to our neighbors' place to have it stored until we come back.

Kimi Tamura

My experience in the evacuation was terrible. After the war went off, the people began to talk about putting us in the camps so we felt unrelieved until we were told to evacuate on a certain day and what to do. After we heard more about the camp and the food and what they were going to do with us in the camp, we were all puzzled up. We didn't know what to do, where to start from, but to keep our heads and do it step by step. We were worried about our home and property until an agent came from the bank to help us. We made arrangements about what to do and all the responsibility. We took his advice and it worked quite well. We did not think of the furniture and we were thinking of storing it in the warehouse. But, the rumors came from all directions. We didn't know what to do again but to take a chance and store it. As we found out later, it is in the safest place to store, so we were relieved. The camp, by hearing from the people there, was much different than the way I heard it. Before coming into the camp the day before, we were so busy that our neighbors came and helped us to pack and load our car. We started off that next morning and it was rainy and muddy. At that moment, I can't forget the parting from my neighbors, who we shared with almost my whole life. When we finally reached our destination, we felt relieved and spent the day sound asleep. The evacuation was the most terrible thing in my whole life.

Roy Yonemura

While going to high school, the most tragic event of all my life happened. Yes, it was the war between America and Japan. I went to school every day until the time for the evacuation. Even after the war broke out, the students were very good to us. Then came the time for evacuation. We sold most of our properties and stored most of our properties, too. When I had to separate from my friends, it brought tears to my eyes. Right before evacuating, one of my teachers came to my house to say good-bye. Even now, she writes to me and she tells me what is happening out at our high school.

Hisako Nada

My experience of the evacuation is something which I shall never forget. One morning in December, I woke up and, to my disappointment, learned that America and Japan had declared war on each other. It was disappointing news, but I didn't dream that the worst was yet to come. When winter rolled by and the beautiful season of spring was rolling in, I began hearing about being evacuated. Being evacuated was something new to me so I was quite excited about it, although I knew that I would never want to leave [the town of] Stockton. One bright day when I came home from school, I received the most shocking news that I ever heard of. It was the order for us to evacuate. The smile which was on my face suddenly passed away and, in its place was a mixture of excitement, confusion, relief, happiness, and sadness, all mixed together. A few days before evacuation, everything was in a mess and we were as busy as ever. The last day finally came and I tried very hard to be cheerful. But when the neighbors came and embraced us in their arms and cried over our leaving, I couldn't help but bawl out like a baby. Evacuation is something which I despise because you are taken away from your dear friends and home.

Evacuees from the West Coast waiting for registration at the Santa Anita Assembly Center; April 1942.
Courtesy of Library of Congress Prints and Photographs Division

Julia Suzuki

December 7. That day I'll never forget! Our friend came to our house and told us that war had begun between America and Japan. We were all shocked because we did not know about it because we were away and did not come home until night. I went to school the next day, feeling smaller than a flea, and wondered what everyone would tell me. But nobody said anything and everyone was friendly. So, I went to school until I had to evacuate.

People interned in Arkansas came mostly from the California assembly centers in Fresno, Stockton, and Santa Anita, where they spent several months before being relocated again. Even after they were in the Arkansas camps, many retained close ties to friends and associates from their assembly centers.

Margaret Samejima

When we woke up to leave for Santa Anita on May 5,

1942, it made me feel as bad as I did on December 7th. I can't describe the feeling I had when we entered the camp. We were given an apartment in the stables and it was so dirty I wanted to cry. The only happiness was probably the many friends I made, but that was soon shattered too with relocation.

Katsumi Sugimoto

In September of 1940, I enrolled at Woodland High School [in Sacramento]. Out of nine hundred students in Woodland High School, one hundred of them are interned in the centers. On May 4, 1942, we moved to the farm by Stockton. We stayed there temporarily until evacuation. Our asparagus farm was taken over by the Caucasians. On May 21, we were evacuated to the Stockton Assembly Center. I worked as a yard laborer for four months. My wage was only eight dollars per month. On October 3, we were sent to Rohwer Relocation Center.

Nellie Utsumi

When we entered Stockton Assembly Center, we were surprised to find that things were better than what we had heard.

Tanji Tashiko

When school was still going on [in California], we had to prepare to evacuate before school had ended. That means we lost quite a bit of lessons, but the teacher gave us homework to do if we wanted the credits. They gave so many days to finish the whole lesson. It was very hot those days but we had to do it, so we did it. We had summer school at the Stockton Assembly Center. We only could take up to three subjects. As the days went by, it was almost time for us to evacuate. We were all excited about where we were to go. Some thought maybe to Colorado, Idaho, Wyoming, Arkansas, New Mexico, or Tule Lake, but finally we heard that we were to be evacuated to Arkansas.

Floyd Ouye

On May 14, 1942, an order came out stating that all Japanese will be evacuated into the Assembly Center by May 21, 1942. We were about the last family to leave Lodi on Thursday at 12:30 in the afternoon. We reached the Assembly Center about 1:00 in the afternoon and were sure disgusted when we saw the barracks. We received help from all of our friends, who had been there for about two days. I immediately went and signed up for any type of work. It was about a week later when I received a notice to report for work in the warehouse under Mr. Harry Morford. I enjoyed working there very much. My rate of pay was $8.00 [a month], which was not very much for this type of work. I made many new friends while working in there. I worked in the warehouse for three months and my time was not wasted. I made so many friends that every time I turn my back, everybody just calls my name.

Trouble at Santa Anita

Although there were very few security problems in the Arkansas camps, many of the people there had seen some unrest in the Santa Anita temporary relocation center before they came to Arkansas. Santa Anita was the only camp in which a serious disturbance took place. On August 4, 1942, a confiscation of hot plates and a search for contraband such as Japanese language books and record albums led to complaints and protests. About 200 military police faced a crowd of 2,000 protestors. Martial law was declared, and camp residents were confined to their barracks for the night. The police withdrew from the camp on August 7 after patrolling for three days. Relations between the inmates of Santa Anita and the management seem to have been worse in that center than in any of the others, possibly because of problems in electing and maintaining inmate representatives.

(Source: Densho Encyclopedia, "Santa Anita: Inmate-Keeper Relations")

Mary Kobayashi

Everyone thought we would be going to Manzanar [a camp at the foot of the Sierra Nevada mountain range in eastern California], but we landed in Santa Anita at the horse-racing track there.

The day we left (April 14) it rained and the going was pretty tough. We left from Downey, California, in a large caravan procession and arrived in Santa Anita after a two-hour ride, feeling very cramped and cross.

The most disappointing thing about Santa Anita was that we lived in stables with no ventilation or privacy whatsoever. All in all, the months spent at the famous racetrack were different and I think I adapted myself to liking it and making the best of the situation. My first graduation was held in the grandstand of Santa Anita, while a school seminar was also held there. Church services were attended by many of the people, who listened to speakers every Sunday among camouflage nets. All was not peace and quiet in this center, for we had this riot which ended disastrously.

Frank Sakioka

It was a cold, cloudy morning when we started off to our destination, Santa Anita Race Track, where Bing Crosby's horse Sea Biscuit used to race.

It was alright being in the camp except for a few troubles

that arose....We had [a riot] on August 4, when the American police force, led by the Koreans, started taking away things that weren't contraband and, besides that, they took money away from some of the barracks when they searched the suitcases. So, I passed the days in Santa Anita until the time came when we had to relocate to Rohwer, Arkansas.

Midori Oura

[War's] dark hand threw an ominous shadow over the Pacific Coast on April 13th, 1942. On that fateful day, I left my blessed home in dear ole Gardena with its invaluable memories and evacuated to the Santa Anita Assembly Center.

Never had we been in a place so devoid of luxuries, and necessities, too. We were assigned a bare horse-stall disguised as a two-roomed unit, whose yet-soft asphalt floor and fresh paint could not alter the pungent odor. The five months dragged themselves slowly by.

Don't Treat Us Like Animals, by Nancy Chikaraishi; "My mother and her family [who ended up at Rohwer in Arkansas] had to live in a horse stall that had been whitewashed by the government. They slept on mattresses filled with hay. During the day they helped in the war effort by making camouflage nets for the army." The text in the background reads in part: You make us live in horse stalls that you whitewash. We sleep on mattresses filled with hay. It's degrading and humiliating. It's shameful that Americans can do this to other American citizens. Would you treat your friends, neighbors or family like this? We are not animals.
Courtesy of Nancy Chikaraishi

Father had always been an ardent news reader. He followed the war news with a practiced eye. My two sisters became school teachers and trudged back and forth over long distances every day. Mother laundered and knitted. I wrote. In between studying for the correspondence course I took to finish my tenth-grade semester, I wrote short stories—mystery stories, humorous stories, and tragedies. The prominent feature of the Santa Anita Assembly Center was the lining-up of people everywhere—in the mess line, the post office, the hospital, the clinic, and many other places. We cracked feeble jokes to keep ourselves smiling, and to keep our minds from dwelling too much on our surroundings.

Marian Yamamoto

On May 6, 1942, we were thrown into the horse stable of Santa Anita Race Track. During my days at Santa Anita, I learned a great deal. I made new friends, had an opportunity to improve my tap dancing, and learned to go to church and Sunday school every Sunday. I also had the great pleasure of teaching tap-dancing. Father came back from camp.

The days went by fast in Santa Anita.

Nagako Horiguchi

The day for us to evacuate had finally come, which was on the date of April 4, 1942. We got up early that morning because we were told to be there at Lawndale at 7 a.m. The day we were evacuated was a very rainy day and we had a hard time keeping our baggage from getting wet. We waited at Lawndale for about two hours before we got started. We left Lawndale at 9 o'clock and finally started to move. I felt very sad and felt like crying because I sure did hate to leave that place that morning. We all drove in a single line while the Army trucks watched us from both sides to see if anything happened to us on the way. We drove really slow that day, especially because it was raining hard. Around 12 o'clock, I was really tired of doing nothing but sitting in the car and looking out the window. Before long, I noticed a sign that read "Santa Anita" and was really glad that we reached our destination safely and before it was dark. It was 12:30 when we reached this place and we missed our noon meal that day. One thing I just didn't like about it when we got there was that we were told to live in the horse stables. I didn't like this room because I felt as though I was a horse being put in a stable. The other thing was that the room smelled awful. After about a week, I got used to this place and I liked it and it felt more like being in a regular house. The first night I slept in this house, I just couldn't sleep because I was homesick and wasn't used to this room. The next day, I woke up feeling fine as usual and was through worrying about being evacuated.

Julia Suzuki

On April 14th, we evacuated to the race track at Santa Anita, which had become an assembly center. Before we left, everyone was saying we could only take a few items of clothing and blankets. We stored some things at a friend's place. We sold our farm to a Mexican man and gave him the things that we left in the house, which was almost everything. We had a hard time getting ready because we did not have a man to help us. When we came to Santa Anita, it was not so bad, but we had to live in a horse stall, and living there was not so comfortable. In Santa Anita, we made many friends but it was very tiresome, and about two months later it was so boring that I learned to knit and knitted a sweater. On August fifth, we were all happy because our father came back from an internment camp in New Mexico.

Tom Saito

On May 6th I entered the great Santa Anita Race Track in Arcadia, California. It is not far from Los Angeles and is right by Pasadena, known for the Rose Bowl. Santa Anita was known for its million-dollar horses which raced down the stretch to the roar of thousands of cheering fans. But a city of 10,000 people had now been built there. The official census later showed that Santa Anita was ranked for three months as the 32nd community in population in California.

Santa Anita had a nickname— Japanita or Santa Tokyo.

The first month in camp went fast for me and the soles of my shoes wore out like they were paper.

In Santa Anita, I had lots of friends and I had all kinds of fun. Once a month, I saw movies and went to lots of dances and talent shows. I played softball, baseball, basketball, and there were lots of other things going on every day.

The bad part came when the camp was split up and sent all over. The city of Eureka will once more become the 32nd city in size in California.

I really miss all my friends. Some of them are in California, Arizona, Wyoming, Colorado, and in our neighbor Jerome, Arkansas.

Walking in Their Shoes
Have you ever been away from home? For a week? Two weeks? More? Can you imagine what it would feel like to not know when you could go home again—or if you ever would?

Mary Takemoto

So, when evacuation came it was quite a relief for everyone and waiting for the day we would be told to "get out," we entered Santa Anita Assembly Center. We didn't have the feeling of being settled either. From here, we would soon be told to "move on."

Nancy Suzuki

We were the last group to move from [the town of] Stockton because we happened to have been left out. So, when the next order came, it included us to evacuate with the Lodi people. Having had a week to get ready, we were now on our way to our new kind of life. Our friends took us to the armory in Lodi and from there we rode Greyhound buses to the Assembly Center in Stockton. Reaching there, we were inspected and then taken to our new homes. My first attitude of the camp wasn't very pleasing but, as time went on, I got so I enjoyed going to school, shows, talent shows, watching baseball games, football and basketball, which if having been at home I never would have had time.

The transfer of evacuees from assembly centers to more permanent camps was conducted by the U.S. Army. Families were not separated, and most groups associated by pre-evacuation residence were kept together. Here, family groups identify hand baggage prior to departure from Santa Anita; 1942.

Courtesy of Library of Congress Prints and Photographs Division

I also had a chance to work as a waitress in our favorite mess hall up to the time of being relocated. The center had a total of about 4,500 people. It was very small compared with other centers. Since it was small, I was able to make many new friends.

In the fall of 1942, the people held at the assembly centers at Santa Anita and Stockton received new orders, this time to move to Arkansas, a place where almost none have them had been—or even knew anything about. They spent days on a train, traveling across the vast expanse of America's west toward Arkansas, a place deemed appropriate for the incarceration of people of Japanese heritage because it was remote from any military targets or activity.

Tom Saito

On October 2nd, the day came when I left the Santa Anita Assembly Center in Arcadia, California, then headed towards the place to which I never dreamed of going.

The day I left the camp, it was a beautiful southern California day. The sun had just come out over the Sierra Madres and high on the grandstand the flag was flying. It was just another day for the people who live on the outside. But, for us, we were going east. First, we went to the city of Los Angeles on the train and went right by the place in which I used to live and play around. As we first came into the city, I saw lots of buildings but as we got in the country we saw lots and lots of that good old California—orange trees and all kinds of farms. Days went by and all we saw were the desert and hills. When we came to Louisiana and Arkansas, there were lots of trees and all kinds of rivers.

The trip took us 5 days and on the 6th morning about 4 o'clock, we got off the train and then good old Rohwer, Arkansas, at last.

Well, I have been here almost two months but I still kind of feel homesick for a little more sunshine.

Nellie Utsumi

Then, [from Stockton] off to Rohwer, Arkansas! The four days' trip was very tiresome. It was the first time I had left California. As we pulled out, tears came out at the thought we might never see it again. Although we had gone through many tragic happenings, we should be thankful to be alive and unharmed.

Floyd Ouye

In September, they told us that we were to be relocated into an unknown relocation center outside of California.

The advance crew was needed, so they asked for the volunteers to make the relocation center ready for the later evacuees. The advance crew was entirely on a voluntary basis, so I signed up and also my two sisters signed up. About two weeks later, it was announced that we were to relocate to Rohwer Relocation Center in Rohwer, Arkansas.

A crowd crosses the football field after a game at Rohwer. Note that several people are carrying pieces of scrap wood. People in the camps often used these materials to build furniture and other items for their barracks. *Courtesy of the UALR Center for Arkansas History and Culture, Life Interrupted Collection; original held by the National Archives and Records Administration*

Many people hated the idea of leaving the good old state of California, which was the birthplace for many of the younger set.

We left good old California with the advance crew on Sept. 14, 1942, for Arkansas. During our train ride, we went through many scenic places like Devil's Pass, the Arizona desert, New Mexico, Colorado, Oklahoma, and Arkansas. We went over the Mississippi River and saw some river barges loaded with sulphur. When we were in Memphis, we were told that we would reach our destination around 10 p.m.

We were all excited to see our new home for the duration. We dropped our diner car off at Memphis, so we did not get to eat our supper on the train. Around 11:05 p.m., when we finally reached the destination, we were greeted by Mr. Ray D. Johnston and Mr. Hiser, Project Director and Housing Dept. Head.

We took our shower and changed to our clean clothes and made our first appearance in Arkansas. Presently, we were called to eat our late supper. Even though it was only a sandwich and water, it was inviting and delicious, thanks to the administrative personnel who were kind enough to go through all the trouble.

After the late supper, I just sat down by my bed and wrote to the friends who were still back in California and will be coming to this center real soon. I was very tired. When I looked at my watch, it read 3 a.m., so I retired for the night. I got up around 7:30 a.m. the next morning and gathered our baggage, which took most of the morning. In the afternoon, I went and got some lumber and made some tables and chairs and a few odd things. That night, they had a meeting and asked for workers for various jobs. I received a job as a hospital warehouse clerk and found the work very interesting. I learned many things about medical supplies and instruments and medicines. My work started from September 21st, 1942, and my pay was double compared to Stockton Assembly Center....I enjoyed working in the warehouse and I would like to get back in there to work again.

First Impressions:

Sam Shimizu, November 18, 1942:

This is a pretty good place but it is too cold sometimes and too hot. The climate and the soil are no comparison with the Lodi [California] weather and soil.

Hiroshi Sato, December 14, 1942:

When I heard we were to be evacuated to Arkansas, you know what I thought? I thought the place was going to be filled with big mosquitoes, it would rain so as to flood the camp, and we would have to be floating on rafts. I also thought there would be rattlesnakes crawling all over. When I came here I found out that my thoughts were all untrue.

Roy Yonemura

Then came the day for us to evacuate once more [from Santa Anita] to the inland. It just so happened that I was relocated to Rohwer Relocation Center, Arkansas. On the way up here, we passed through many states. From morning to night, I gazed out the window and saw the beautiful scenery.

After arriving here, I tried to adjust myself to the environment in Arkansas, but it is pretty hard to really get used to the climate. Up to now, I tried to make myself as happy as I could be by making a lot of new friends.

Nancy Suzuki

I left Stockton, California, on October 3, 1942, on a train, which was my first trip by train. Never having ridden on a train before, I enjoyed my trip very much. The route we took was through the southern states such as Arizona, New Mexico, Texas, and then Arkansas. Having arrived here, I found this place very enjoyable. Never having lived out of California, I am finding this a very new experience.

Tanji Tashiko

When the final day [at Stockton] came, we had a car number and the date when we were to leave. A man checked our name by the gate and we walked down the street with our baggage in hand until we reached the train. We came on a Southern Pacific train, passing through Los Angeles, California, Arizona, New Mexico, Texas, and then to Arkansas. On our way, I practically only saw shrubs and desert until we came into Arkansas. Here, I saw many, many beautiful, green trees and many beautiful but unfamiliar stones. I sure wanted to have some!

Arkansas is a very nice place. It is very similar to California except the weather is a little different because it seems every time it is going to rain it gets warmer, but in California, it is the opposite.

Arkansas is a very nice place to live in. I think I am always going to like it.

Mary Takemoto

So, finally, when we were told we would have to come to Arkansas, we were quite pleased for we knew this would be for the duration of the war. But even today everything is quite uncertain. So, about the only thing is to keep in the best spirit possible and to look forward to a possible "brighter tomorrow."

Mary Kobayashi

It seems that everything does not run smoothly on the road to life. There are the ups

Children have a snowball fight at Jerome.
Courtesy of the UALR Center for Arkansas History and Culture, Life Interrupted Collection

and downs. Just as we were getting used to [Santa Anita] and having ice cream every Sunday, another evacuation notice was posted. Again, hectic days followed and leaving our new-found friends was harder yet. Saying goodbye to them early in the morning through a barbed-wire fence and waiting until the train pulled out and seeing the silently weeping ones made a lump in my throat.

The day arrived when we said goodbye to everyone and saw for the last time the horse barracks all in a row and turned our faces toward the south to Rohwer, Arkansas. The trip was long and tiresome, although some of the states had some pretty scenery. When I sighted Rohwer, I was dusty, tired and hot, but tremendously happy to see the center, and I personally believe it's one of the best.

A number of evacuees said in their 1942 autobiographies that the weather in Arkansas was much like the weather in California, so they felt right at home. No doubt they were disappointed (and chilled) as rainy weather and then the cold Arkansas winter set in. The rain turned the already swampy ground at the camps to mud. But many of the young people got to experience their first snowstorm while in Arkansas.

Marian Yamamoto

Time came for us to evacuate to the relocation center.... For the first time in my life, I took a long trip on a train. It was very uncomfortable on the train and sure tiresome. At night, there were four of us sleeping together on the seat. We came through Arizona, New Mexico, Texas, Louisiana, and then to the relocation center in Arkansas. It was the first time I ever went out of California. This camp was a million times better than I expected. We all are glad we came here.

This will be my home until this mess is over and I hope it will be over soon. I know I'll get used to Arkansas like I was at California. Our family are all together now and we're getting along just fine.

Midori Oura

After five dreary months [at Santa Anita], we received notice that we were being relocated in Arkansas. However far Arkansas may have seemed to us, in our hearts we were glad that we were going to a permanent relocation center [for the duration of the war].

Julia Suzuki

Then on September 22, we got notice to evacuate for the second time. We were to come to Arkansas. I was very sorry

I had to go because many of my friends were still there. But, I was kind of happy to leave Santa Anita too because this was the first time I was to be out of California. I boarded the train for the first time knowing I would be in another camp soon. We were on the train for four days and nights. We went through the states of Arizona, New Mexico, Texas, and Louisiana. I enjoyed the train trip very much and wished I could ride on a train again.

Camp isn't so fun, and when I hear from the outside, I feel like I want to be out there all the more.

Lillian Hananouchi

The trip [to Rohwer] wasn't exciting for me because I became so sick I didn't care where I was going. The first day here was a sunny day, which made me homesick for California because it was always sunny there. After a few weeks, I disliked it more for it was always raining, which made mud here and there and the house was so hard to keep clean. It has been over two months since I came here and I'm hoping they do something about the mud.

Margaret Samejima

When they all left [Santa Anita] for other centers other than Rohwer I wanted to leave too.

We were overcrowded on the train. At night it was especially bad. The first two nights I didn't sleep but took naps between meals. The food on the train was the best I had tasted in months. The scenery was too monotonous to be interesting.

High school students change classes on muddy ground at Rohwer Relocation Center; November 1942.
Courtesy of the UALR Center for Arkansas History and Culture, Life Interrupted Collection; original held by the National Archives and Records Administration

We arrived on a very chilly morning. Somehow I felt relieved. Rohwer is so much nicer than Santa Anita but slowly its bad points are appearing too. I've started to make friends all over again. I know I'm going to go through another parting when resettlement comes but somehow I have come to the conclusion that I can't think of the past or the future either. All I can do is live the days as they come, good or bad.

Chapter 2
Voices: American, Un-American, and Everything in Between

The young people who found themselves in the camps in Arkansas were very much in a state of being "in between"—between childhood and adulthood, and between the more traditional Japanese life of their parents and the life of younger Americans. Their old life in California was behind them, while their future as American adults (uncertain as it was) lay before them. They were stalled, with their engines idling.

And one complicated question followed them through the gates into the camps: Does the fact that I was born in America make me an American—not just by law but by actual perception and practice? Even more complex questions follow: What makes people American? Looking a certain way? Holding a certain legal status? Abiding by the U.S. Constitution? Fitting in? Contributing to American society in some way?

Many people in Arkansas viewed the Japanese Americans with suspicion, based mostly on how they looked—their facial features, anyway. The residents of the small towns brought fear and prejudice to their encounters with the people of Japanese ancestry who showed up in their poor, fairly isolated part of the world, in part because the nation was at war with Japan and in part due to unfamiliarity with foreign cultures. As author David Robson stated, "As the trains carrying Japanese Americans and their extended families arrived in Jerome, hundreds—both black and white—stood to watch. Yet they were not there to welcome the new arrivals; instead, they came to get a look at the strangers who would be living among them."[1]

Arkansas was typical of the rest of America at the time in its racist attitudes toward Asians—attitudes that intensified during the war. (Images in popular culture during the war, from Bugs Bunny cartoons to comic books to movies, reinforced those attitudes.) Another complication was the fact that China was an ally to America during World War II, while Japan was an enemy. About two weeks after the bombing of Pearl Harbor, *LIFE* magazine published an article titled, "How to Tell Japs from the Chinese: Angry Citizens Victimize Allies with Emotional Outburst at Enemy." The article, which was illustrated with annotated photographs of Chinese and Japanese people, stated: "In the first discharge of emotions touched off by the Japanese assaults on their nation, U.S. citizens have been demonstrating a distressing ignorance on the delicate question of how to tell a Chinese from a Jap. Innocent victims in cities all over the country are many of the 75,000 U.S. Chinese, whose homeland is our [staunch] ally.... To dispel some of this confusion, LIFE here adduces a rule-of-thumb from the anthropometric conformations that distinguish friendly Chinese from enemy alien Japs."[2] Implicit in this message, of course, is that violence directed at those of Japanese ancestry was okay, or at least understandable.

When the Japanese Americans arrived in Arkansas, they were also met with jealously and resentment, which seems odd at first. Is an American who has been unjustly uprooted and incarcerated a person to be jealous of? But, as the locals in the towns of Rohwer and Jerome and the surrounding area saw it, the internees had things they themselves did not always have: a hospital, plenty of food, electricity, running water, and so on. This area of Arkansas, inhabited by sharecroppers and tenant farmers (farmers who did not own their land), had not yet recovered from the Great Depression of the 1930s.

The young people in the camps were very aware of the way they were viewed by the Arkansas citizens. As Rohwer High School art teacher Mabel Rose Jamison (later Vogel) said very poignantly of one of her students:

> One of my dear high school senior girls came to me and said, "Miss Jamison, I have a problem, and it's worrying me, and I don't know what to do about it." And she looked at me with her big brown eyes, and she looked so pained, and she said, "Miss Jamison, I'm an American. I was born here. And I want to be just as good an American citizen as you are. But what am I gonna do about these Japanese eyes?"[3]

Walking in Their Shoes
Were you born in the United States? Were your parents? Were your grandparents? Are you an American citizen? Do you ever think about what that means? Do you think you should be treated in a different way from someone who is not a citizen, or whose parents are not citizens? Do you think there is "liberty and justice for all" in America today?

Even before being sent to Arkansas during World War II, young Nisei (born in America to Japanese parents, the Issei) had grappled with similar questions. They sometimes faced racism in their communities, a continuation of racism that had persisted ever since Chinese and Japanese immigrants had begun arriving in the 1800s to find work in America—with a new wave of Japanese arriving around the early 1900s, the Issei. Some Nisei felt ashamed of their Issei parents who held strongly to Japanese traditions and often tried to shut themselves off from wider American society. Rebelling against their parents' attitudes, many young people worked hard to fit in with their white peers. Some, however, avoided white schoolmates and worked doubly hard on schoolwork, hoping that getting a good education would smooth their way into a successful American adulthood.

It is interesting also to note that many of the Japanese American students' white schoolmates in California could have heritage matching one of the United States' other enemies during the war, such as Italy and Germany. One wonders why—besides a long history of racial discrimination against Asians—this boy's Italian and German American playmates were not attacked or sent to camps:

Frank Sakioka
I had to quit school because of the evacuation, which was a very sad thing to do. I really did enjoy school, with English, Italian, German, and French boys to play with, for they, too, were Americans, just as I.

Regarding the young people who found themselves in the Arkansas camps in the 1940s, Arkansas author and poet John Gould Fletcher wrote, "The generation from fourteen to eighteen, now passing through the high school at the Rohwer

Camp, are, as anyone who has seen them must admit, perfectly Americanized. These girls with their permanent waves, their bobby-socks, these boys with their sweaters, their looks, casual swinging gait—are, except for facial characteristics, not oriental at all."[4]

The Japanese American students themselves were well aware that some people felt they were racially inferior to whites because of their Japanese features, and they wanted to try to get past that type of prejudice. As an editorial written by a high school senior in Jerome's high school student publication *The Condensor* said, "Occidental [i.e., European or white] Americans may at times discriminate against you, but do not lose sight of the fact that America does not signify physical racial traits but a way of living and thinking. And for those who cannot see thus, you should be the ones to elucidate what it means to be an American."[5]

One of the central goals of the camp school curriculum was to instill in the students a knowledge of and adherence to American ideals, such as freedom and democracy. As Beryl Henry, the curriculum director of the Jerome Relocation Center, said, "Because a child is a citizen we believe we must lead him to regard his school as a Community in which he lives and one in which he may be useful and happy....Goals and outposts must be firmly placed to indoctrinate the child in the fundamental principles of Democracy."[6] The irony of this statement is that most of the young people already had a very firm grasp of American ideals—enough of a grasp to realize that their incarceration did not match up with the very ideals of freedom and citizenship espoused by their teachers. As historian Jan Ziegler put it, "Many of these young people may have ended the internment experience far less convinced than previously that they belonged to America or that America belonged to them."[7]

Girls' basketball team with their coach at Rohwer.
Courtesy of the Butler Center for Arkansas Studies, Edna A. Miller Collection

As historian Lane Ryo Hirabayashi pointed out, the schools "constituted a racially segregated educational system controlled by the U.S. government," making it impossible for the schools to be run in a democratic manner.[8] It is important to note that *all* American schools were racially segregated at this time, with African American students attending separate schools from white students. This would not change until the U.S. Supreme Court's decision in *Brown v. Board of Education of Topeka* in 1954, nearly a decade after World War II ended.

The young people had already learned about the U.S. Constitution and the rights and protections it offered to American citizens, and they thought about their incarceration in terms of democracy and constitutionality.

Roy Kanuda

Evacuation wasn't necessary to me. I guess we have to make the best of it....I hope the war ends quickly so we could go home. Some of my friends said it was unconstitutional. I hope the bad feelings will go away when we get home.

Takeo Shibata

When this war started and all the Japanese people, alien and citizen, were ordered off the Pacific coast it was a shock to me. There I was, just out of eighth grade, where I was taught that the Constitution guarded all the rights of its citizens. I had to forget all that was taught to me about our democratic country. I cannot put into words the feeling I had when we had to sell our furniture. To see another man, smiling, drive our new car away, forever!...I hope in the near future we will be able to go outside and lead a life like we used to in Los Angeles, to lead a life like any other red-blooded American.

Rohwer High School students on their way to class; November 1942. *Courtesy of the UALR Center for Arkansas History and Culture, Life Interrupted Collection; original held by the National Archives and Records Administration*

Himi Hashimoto

When we were all going to schools somewhere in California we were all happy going on as everyday school, church, and etc. Having fun with our American friends outside. Well, on December 7th when the war was declared I didn't know what to do because I thought that my friends wouldn't want to play with me on account of this war against

46

Japan. I did not want to go to school the next day. Thought I would not be wanted. But as I thought it over and over again I said to myself, Himi, Why should you stay home? You are an American-Japanese citizen just as well as anyone else. Got brave again 'cause I was proud to be an American. When I went back to school the next day everyone was the same only much nicer....And I'm glad to say that I am an American citizen and will always stick up for the Stars and Stripes which I was raised under. I am proud of that. America is my desire and not Japan even if my parents were born there.

Joanne Nogochi

On December the seventh, when war broke out, our hearts stood still. How would our neighbors take it? What about school? Would they understand that we, as Americans, were just as shocked and angry as they were? Would they take anything out on our parents, who were not American citizens, not that they didn't want to be? We should have known better than to have even thought that they would understand how hard it was to have one country as home yet be a race of another. Then we realized that it wasn't a war of people against people, but country against country. And which is my country? America, of course. On Monday, December eighth, all my classmates gave me an extra special smile, showing that they understood and believed in me. It made tears come to my eyes.

Yoshiman Sugimoto

When I first heard that we might be evacuated from the West Coast, I thought we had just as much privilege as other people, but then I didn't consider what every loyal citizen should. Democracy comes first. When the evacuation started, there were no busier people in the world than the Japanese. They were every place a fellow could think of. Dry goods store, Banks, Equipment Co., etc. "What did you get for your equipment? How was the arrangement?"...These words were heard everywhere. If it wasn't [for] the Christian organization, I think Japanese would have lost more than the sum of $100,000,000.00, which was figured out a little while ago...

Would we be accepted after the war? Maybe we would now because of the manpower shortage, but I think a fellow with common horse sense would accept us after the war. When I heard that we are to clean up a forest of 10,000 acres, I thought we are going to be pioneers again. In California, we Japanese established one of the richest delta lands in the world. Are we going to do it again?

Some young people also grappled with the question of exactly who was being protected by their relocation—were the other Americans being protected from them or were they themselves being protected?

Fusaye Sagata

In the Santa Anita assembly center [before coming to Rohwer], I met many people from all walks of life and all of whom were in the same situation as I—unwanted by the people outside. At least that was our lone bitter thought then. Later after considering the whole thing, we came to realize that our way of thinking was incorrect—it meant merely that we are confined to camps for our own protection. However, it was not easy to realize that.

In some ways, being in the camps made the people held there less in tune with what was going on in wartime America as a whole.

Margaret Kataoka

I have already tasted a little of "outside life" and I love it. It seems to take me to the more real side of life and much closer to the war. You feel it everywhere you go....When I go shopping I realize much easier the scarcity of the various articles, whereas in camp it is a little harder to realize because almost all necessary shopping is done through the mail....When shopping for groceries, we also find that a lot of vegetables are scarce because of the scarcity of farm laborers because so many of them have been drafted or are working higher paying jobs in defense plants. We also find another reason for the scarcity is the need of sending so great a portion of our food abroad to our fighting men and to the captured nations. We in camp are less apt to think of these things because we are "inside." Some of us hardly realize the scarcity of some goods because the government does all the shopping for us. I want to go "outside" before the war is over because I believe I should at least get a bigger idea as to what is going on out there and exactly how much the American people are sacrificing to win this war. After all of this (the war and camp life) is over I want to be able to tell the future generation a great deal about the American sacrifices and the conditions here and there. I know I cannot do this unless I can go out and take the whole thing in, by seeing real things before my very eyes....I know I am living in the midst of a great and important part of American history as well as world history and I feel I truly don't want to miss out on as much of this as I can possibly help.[9]

The isolation of the camps and excess of free time also made the people held in the camps adhere more to traditional Japanese ways of thinking and living. Thus, collecting all the people of Japanese descent together in the camps in a way they had not generally been before the war had the undesired effect (to the American government anyway) of reviving and reinforcing traditional Japanese activities, such as traditional dance, music, and artwork. Many young people could explore these activities, particularly artwork, in the camps in a way they never had the time or inclination to before. But, as historian Lane Hirabayashi pointed out in analyzing the effects of internment on Nisei schoolchildren, "One contradiction [in the camps' educational system] was the natural product of the forced Americanization process that required Japanese Americans to put a negative value on everything related to the Japanese culture and tradition, even the many positive elements."[10] It was no doubt difficult to maintain a justifiable pride in Japanese heritage while kept in a camp because of this very heritage.

Although some beautiful artwork was created amid these troubled times, internment created a situation of government dependence, isolated people from the rest of the country, broke down family structures, and fostered racial tensions.

On the other hand, as Hirabayashi said, "As a result of these contradictions [in the education process at the camps]

Loyalty Questionnaire

In 1943, the War Department and the War Relocation Authority created a way to determine so-called loyalty in the camps. All the adults were asked to answer questions on what became known as the "loyalty questionnaire." Most of the questions related to identifying family members, past places of residence, educational levels, language skills, religion, recreational activities, memberships in associations, and family members and/or property in Japan. These questions seemed simple enough, but they were scored according to categories of "Americanness" and "Japaneseness" indicated by each response.

The most controversial questions asked whether a person's birth had been registered in Japan and if a person had renounced his or her Japanese citizenship, would serve in combat duty if ordered, and would declare loyalty to the United States and renounce allegiance to the emperor of Japan. Responses were meant to aid in recruiting young men into an all-Nisei combat unit and authorizing others for resettlement outside of the camps. Those who were found to be "disloyal" because of their answers on the questionnaire were segregated at the high-security Tule Lake camp in California, which eventually became overcrowded.

The badly administered program provoked resistance and resentment over unconstitutional wartime treatment.

(Sources: Densho Encyclopedia, "Loyalty Questionnaire" and "Segregation")

A young Japanese American folk dancer provides outdoor entertainment at Rohwer. *Courtesy of the UALR Center for Arkansas History and Culture, Life Interrupted Collection; original held by the National Archives and Records Administration*

A second-grade class at Rohwer celebrates Thanksgiving.
Courtesy of the UALR Center for Arkansas History and Culture, Life Interrupted Collection

many Nisei responded to the traumas of the war and the forced internment by trying to become 110 percent American. Surrounded by a hostile society doubting Japanese American affiliations and loyalties, many Nisei responded with a strategy of aggressive assimilation to dominant society norms."[11]

Throughout the war, patriotic celebrations were held in the camps, just as they were held everywhere in America.

But how better to show oneself to be a true American than by serving in the U.S. armed forces? Many young Japanese Americans did just that, although some were reluctant.

As one internee said, rather wryly, on February 8, 1943: "A call for Nisei volunteers into the U.S. Army [is] issued. A special combat unit is to be organized. Boy, how suddenly they put things like that before us. Propaganda will be to good purpose—isn't that making us stomach all the sacrifices and no breaks? What of post war status? Where do Nisei soldiers 'go home'—suppose enough

Artwork created at Rohwer.
Courtesy of the Butler Center for Arkansas Studies

Young Japanese American girls at the Jerome Relocation Center.
Courtesy of the Arkansas History Commission

don't volunteer—they sure put us on the spot."[12]

There were enough volunteers, however, and they served their country well. Author David Robson stated that, after the war,

On July 15, 1946, [President Harry] Truman spoke to the 100th Battalion and 442nd Regimental Combat Team made up of young Japanese Americans, most [of] whom had spent some time in internment camps. In his remarks, Truman reflected on the soldiers' battle not only against American enemies but also American intolerance. The speech reflected the stunning turnaround of a government that until recently had eyed these soldiers and their families with suspicion. "I can't tell you how much I appreciate the opportunity to tell you what you have done for this country," said Truman. "You fought not only the enemy, but you fought prejudice. And you won. You have made the Constitution stand for what it really means: the welfare of all the people, all the time."[13]

Celebration of the Obon Odori Festival at Rohwer, summer 1943 or 1944. This is a Japanese Buddhist custom that honors ancestors. Notable is the contrast between the traditional Japanese kimonos and the American-style outfits.
Courtesy of the UALR Center for Arkansas History and Culture, Life Interrupted Collection

After the war ended in 1945, however, many of the people who had been held in the camps did not know how they now fit into American society, which was still segregated by race, especially in the South. Schools, organizations, and modes of transportation had written and unwritten codes applying to people of different races. For instance, many buses had segregated seating, with white people and black people sitting in separate sections.

Where did Japanese Americans sit on the bus? Former Rohwer internee Ben Tsutomu Chikaraishi, who was twenty-one years old when he entered camp, faced that question after he was released:

> I got on the bus and my first decision I had to make outside of camp was "Where do I sit?" The white people sat in the front of the bus. The blacks were in the back. And so I got on and I thought, "Gee, I don't know where should I sit?" So I said, "Gee, we were confined for so long and we were discriminated [against] so much that maybe I'll be considered black," so I went to and I sat in the black area. The bus driver stopped the bus and he says, "Hey, you gotta sit in the front." So I got up and moved, but I didn't come way in the front either. I sat right by the dividing line.[14]

It would take the civil rights movement of the 1950s and 1960s to put an end to this kind of officially sanctioned racial segregation in America and the confusion and heartbreak that came with it.

A sign placed in the window of a store in Oakland, California, on December 8, 1941, the day after the bombing of Pearl Harbor; photo taken March 1942. The store was closed following evacuation orders. The owner, a University of California graduate, was interned for the duration of the war.
Courtesy of Library of Congress Prints and Photographs Division

Notes

1. David Robson, *The Internment of Japanese Americans* (San Diego, CA: ReferencePoint Press, Inc., 2014), 43–44.

2. *LIFE* magazine, December 22, 1941, 81–82.

3. "Rohwer," *Arkansas Traveler*, AETN, 1990, 60-430, Arkansas Humanities Council, Little Rock, Arkansas, quoted in Jan Fielder Ziegler, *The Schooling of Japanese American Children at Relocation Centers During World War II: Miss Mabel Jamison and Her Teaching of Art at Rohwer, Arkansas* (Lewiston, NY: The Mellen Press, 2005), 143.

4. John Gould Fletcher, "East Goes West in Arkansas," *Asia and the Americas* (December 1944): 538, quoted in Ziegler, *The Schooling of Japanese American Children*, 116.

5. Quoted in Ziegler, *The Schooling of Japanese American Children*, 133.

6. Smith-Thompson Papers, "Philosophy for School Curriculum," Beryl Henry, Curriculum Director, Jerome Relocation Center, Roll 3, quoted in Ziegler, *The Schooling of Japanese American Children*, 49.

7. Jan Fielder Ziegler, "Listening to 'Miss Jamison': Lessons from the

Schoolhouse at a Japanese Internment Camp, Rohwer Relocation Center," *Arkansas Review: A Journal of Delta Studies* 33 (August 2002): 145.

8. Lane Ryo Hirabayashi, "The Impact of Incarceration on the Education of Nisei Schoolchildren," in *Japanese Americans: From Relocation to Redress*, ed. Roger Daniels, Sandra C. Taylor, and Harry H. L. Kitano (Salt Lake City: University of Utah Press, 1986), 48.

9. Margaret Kataoka student essay, December 19, 1944, from the journal of Mabel Rose Jamison, quoted in Ziegler, *The Schooling of Japanese American Children*, 130–31.

10. Hirabayashi, "The Impact of Incarceration," 48.

11. Hirabayashi, "The Impact of Incarceration," 48.

12. Excerpts from Diary of Evacuee, Rohwer Relocation Center, McGehee, Arkansas, Austin Smith Papers, MG04350, Arkansas History Commission, Little Rock, Arkansas.

13. Robson, *The Internment of Japanese Americans*, 66.

14. Courtesy of Ben Tsutomu Chikaraishi and Nancy Chikaraishi.

As these young people in the camps confronted the question of their place in America, they also faced a related question: What is my place in my family? Many of these young Japanese Americans had extended family in Japan or in Japanese communities in Hawaii (Hawaii was a U.S. territory at this time, becoming a state in 1959). Some had traveled to visit these relatives, sometimes for a year or more, giving them a unique experience as a stranger in a strange land—but which land was the strange one?

Many students at Rohwer wrote in their 1942 English-class autobiographies about trips to Japan.

Elsie Komura

I had to stand a week of sea-sickness on the trip to Japan. The nature of my trip was to visit and meet my relatives. Looking over the boat rail, we saw the island of Hawaii. When we anchored in the port, music was playing and from little girls to old, the ladies were selling leis. People of Hawaii that we never knew before greeted us. Some of our friends brought us to see the sights. We sailed at dawn.

In reaching the port of Japan, the place did not look any different as those of America. An experience in Japan was most embarrassing! Forgetting the Japanese customs of taking my shoes off, I ran into the hotel. People of the hotel just gasped and looked at me as though I committed a terrible crime. That was Lesson One, but I soon found out that there were many more lessons to come. The building had escalators and elevators. Having been used to the American food, I had a hard time eating the things they cooked and served. I certainly was homesick for America. A year later, I came back and landed in the harbor of San Francisco. I had come back alone, for my grandparents had stayed back and built a home.

Henry Hiroto

I traveled to Japan—that was the first long trip. We made many small trips. I do not remember very much of the first trip to Japan. The second trip I made to Japan I can recall because it was only five or four years ago. It was in the year of 1937, month of May, when we left the land ready to leave the harbor. They threw tapes (streamers) to us when the gong for leaving rang. Everybody was yelling good-bye and bidding farewell to their friends, parents, cousins, etc. I hated to see my friend's face disappearing into fog. After we left the harbor, all we could see was the ocean all over. The ship started to rock a little. The next morning, I saw seagulls tailing us and flying fish jumping out of the water. We were sailing quietly when we saw the school of whales. We had many games to play on the ship. I learned how to play ping pong on the ship. We reached Hawaii on the fifth day. We got off for a 14-hour leave. We had friends by this time. We went to see the pretty places of Hawaii with them. We went to Waikiki beach. The first thing we saw in America again was the same thing except from the opposite side. We got on the ship. It stopped by Hawaii as most of the ships do. It was 2 a.m. in the morning when we saw the light on the Golden Gate Bridge and the Bay Bridge light in a far distance away. After we got off, we went to the World's Fair to look around and then headed back to [the town of] Stockton again. We had a fair trip going back and forth.

Martial Law in Hawaii

People of Japanese heritage made up about a third of Hawaii's population when World War II began. The government's doubts about this large population's loyalty to the United States during a war with Japan became the primary justification for putting the entire territory of Hawaii under military law. Mass removal was impractical, however, as Japanese labor was essential to Hawaii and shipping was unavailable. So, the army instituted a policy of "selective internment," allowing most Japanese Americans to live in their own homes (and in most cases, continue their prewar employment). A relatively small number were relocated to centers in Hawaii and then camps on the mainland, such as Jerome in Arkansas. Hawaii's entire civilian and alien population was under army rule from December 1941 to October 1944. (Source: Densho Encyclopedia, "Martial Law in Hawaii")

Emiko Taguchi

[On the way to Japan on a ship last year] we passed many small islands, like Midway Island. And finally on the twentieth of July, we saw land again! We were in Yokohama, Japan. We reached Yokohama on a rainy day. My grandfather was waiting for us, so after everything was inspected, we got off the boat and went to a hotel in Yokohama. The first thing I noticed was to take my shoes off before I got into the house. When bed-time came, the hotel furnished us blankets and quilts and we slept on the mat floor. We were used to the food because we liked rice the best. Then after leaving Yokohama, I noticed again that people walked on the left side of the street. Then we went on the train to my mother's native town. It took us about three days. When we reached the station, every face was somebody I didn't know. I went [to the beach] real early in the morning and what do you suppose I saw? I saw the sun coming up from the ocean which is the east and setting in the west like we see here. But, only in America I used to see the sun coming up east, as it is supposed to be but the sun setting in the ocean in the west. It really seems peculiar to me.

After about a month of rest, I started school in Japan. I made many friends, but when the time came for me to leave my friends, I really felt like I had to leave back something precious. About after four months of vacation, we decided to go back to America. When I got in the boat again, I thought, is this a dream or only a voyage? My first time to believe there was a land called Japan.

Kimi Tamura

My father was a farmer since I was born. He farmed with my grandparents before they went back to their home land of Japan. My mother helped them farm, too. My mother taught me to obey her until now. Every time I did something wrong, she always caught me and told me not to do it. One thing I will not forget is throwing mud on my younger sister's eyes. She cried loudly so my mother came running and shouting, "What's wrong?" I didn't answer but she saw it. Did she give me a lecture then! I was about ten or eleven years old. Mother taught me how to sing because she loves music, too. I still remember some of the songs she taught me.

We have six people in our family. I have three sisters. I do not have any brothers. My big sister is studying in Japan. She went there a couple of years before the war broke out to live with my grandparents. They are now living in their new home in Japan. I will never forget their parting with us until some day we meet again.

With the strong ties many of these young people had to relatives in Japan, it is poignant to think about how the war affected both of their worlds: Japanese and American. It is especially heartbreaking when they mention family members who lived in Hiroshima or Nagasaki—cities on which the Americans dropped devastating atomic bombs in 1945 to help bring about the surrender of Japan that ended World War II.

Nobuo Tomito

My grandfather's name is Kametaro Tomita and he was once a great Samurai (a warrior) and is now living in Furuta-mura Hiroshima, Japan. He is now 98 years old and his wife is 92. Both of them still have lots of life left in them.

What was once a cohesive family experience—worship—also seemed to be in flux in the families at this time, with many of the older generations as Shinto or Buddhist and the younger generation becoming Christian, the predominant religion of the United States. As camps encouraged Christian worship as part of Americanization, it is probable that internment sped along some of these changes, which were already well under way when the war started.

Kimi Tamura

My parents' religion comes from generations to generations, even if they did not want to be. They are Shinto. Which is the god for Japan from long ago. It is like worshipping Christ, as we do. My sister and I are Protestants since last year. We went to a small country church in our district near our home. The teacher was sent down by the pastors to help us. We went there every Saturday and Sunday. The smallest sister sang, younger sister played the piano, and I played the violin, so they called us the "three sisters." We had quite a time there.

Photograph depicting a wood carving of the Buddha by Harry G. Koizumi; Rohwer, Arkansas, 1945.
Courtesy of the Butler Center for Arkansas Studies, Rosalie Santine Gould–Mabel Jamison Vogel Collection

Hiroko Yasutake

My father is a Christian and my mother was a Buddhist. My sisters and brothers all went to the Buddhist church except me. I went to the Christian church when I was seven years old. I quit going at the age of twelve in order to help on the farm.

Midori Oura

One of my closest girlfriends [in California] was a devout Christian. I, myself, had been a Buddhist—or, shall I say, I attended a Buddhist Church for a year when I was a tiny tot, but I ceased to go because I could not understand their ways. After that, I did not step inside a church, except at rare intervals, until a month before evacuation. My friend had urged me to attend her Baptist church. And finally, when the church was celebrating the "Seven Great days" for young people in Gardena, I decided to go. The minister and what he said made a powerful impression on me. I could see that my sisters were influenced, too.

Nancy Suzuki

My religion is Christian and I am a member of the Methodist church. The church, as a whole, is very strict. At the Assembly

Center, I attended the Young People's services. In Rohwer, I attend the Young People's services and Young People's Fellowship. Everyone has his own type of church but being in here, all the Christians are members of the Rohwer Federated Protestant Church.

Shagao Hamada

I believe in Buddhism. I always went to church on Saturdays with the folks. They had a shrine in Los Angeles, so we always used to go there. After camp, I never went.

While many families went to the internment camps as a family unit, many were also scattered for various reasons.

Hiroko Yasutake

There were ten members in the family but there are seven of us now. My mother passed away on May 20, 1942, one month after we got in Santa Anita Assembly Center. My oldest brother was drafted into the army in January of 1941 and is a staff sergeant. He will be going overseas in a week. My oldest sister is married and living in Poston Relocation Center [in Arizona]. I have all together five brothers and two sisters.

While the War Relocation Authority recognized that the incarceration of Japanese Americans would have some negative effects on family life, it hoped that the young people would be a positive force for improving the attitude and outlook of their parents. In her book *The Schooling of Japanese Americans*, historian Jan Ziegler quotes some WRA documents that illuminate this idea of schools helping the students in turn help their parents "outgrow the shock of evacuation and relocation." It was hoped that the schools would:

> aid in developing a desirable community spirit and morale. Many evacuees resented evacuation and had little interest in project community life. With mess hall feeding, living in cramped quarters, and with no family

Children receiving Easter baskets; Rohwer Relocation Center, 1944.
Courtesy of the Butler Center for Arkansas Studies, Edna A. Miller Collection

enterprises, and with few home obligations or duties for the children parental control lagged. These conditions and a lack of home duties and obligations on the part of the child provided a natural setting for the development of group activities and gangs....With a partial breakdown of home life school officials recognized a definite need for extending the school services to pick up a part of this lag in pupil education.[1]

One major element of camp life that was different from the home lives the internees had left was the communal eating in mess halls rather than with their families, as had been done back in California. Gone were the traditional family meals of food of a family's choosing eaten together with proper manners.

Walking in Their Shoes

Think about how your family would deal with the stress of relocation. Could you share close quarters peacefully? Would you eat together? How might family roles and dynamics shift?

Takeo Shibata

When I first sat down to eat at a long wooden table with thousands of other evacuees [at an assembly center in Arcadia, California] I saw some people with tears in their eyes as they started to eat the poor meal, out of metal plates. I guess they all felt like I did for they hardly touched their plates and kept their heads bent down. This was the first meal. Later they seemed to get used to the eating with thousands of other people, for they started to talk to friends across the table and beside them.

Chiyoko Tahara

During dinner times, I didn't care to eat with other families because I didn't know what other people may think of my manners, for it was the first time I ate with forks. I always used to eat with chop sticks. But I got used to using a fork.

George Kobayashi

One thing I truly miss is our Thanksgiving and Christmas dinners. I can still picture the delicious roast turkey, stuffing, ice cream, cranberries, pumpkin pie, and all the other goodies that my mother made for us.

From the diary of a young woman held at the Rohwer camp, December 14, 1942[2]:

People's table manners have ceased to exist. When older people grab and reach all over the table, children can't be expected to retain fine manners. It's a case of grab or starve. Milk for children only and, yet, certain older people demand it. Menus are predominantly starch. Pork is the only kind of meat and it gives us hives.

From a teenager's perspective, though, this system had both its downsides (no more home-cooked meals) and its upsides (being able to eat with friends).

Kazuko "Kaz" (Tsubouchi) Fujishima—one of the teen girls pictured on the truck at Jerome on the cover of this book—said this about the dining situation in a 2003 interview:

> When we went into camp, there was a separation in families, and I do feel that our father did not have control of us as much as he did on the outside, and so life was much easier for us girls [laughs], I must say. So, we were supposed to eat as a family unit, but us teenagers all got together and ate together, and the parents would sit with their friends and eat together with them, so the family unit was broken, actually, when we went into camps.[3]

Despite all the family strife caused by internment—coupled with the normal disharmony often experienced between teenagers and their parents—warm and respectful feelings for their family members come through very strongly in the students' autobiographies.

Nancy Kiriu

A mother is the most understanding person in the world, especially to a growing girl. She assists us in doing the right thing at the correct time. Oftentimes she would scold me, but I know that she is doing it only to help me. I was taught how to cook and sew and also how to keep house. I think I am very fortunate to have both a father and a mother, for they are more precious than gold. My mother had often taught me how to crochet, but it was not until we went to the assembly center that I became interested in it, and it is now my favorite hobby.

Everyday Life in Rohwer
"Rain is nice—keeps the dust down. Victory gardens progressing, snakes are coming out of hibernation in the woods. It's a Rohwer custom to walk about with your nose to the ground—it may not improve your posture but you might find an agate, or some stone suitable for polishing. Other people with leisure time go cray-fishing with nets along the ditches."
(Source: Excerpts from Diary of Evacuee, Rohwer Relocation Center, McGehee, Arkansas, Austin Smith Papers, MG04350, Arkansas History Commission, Little Rock, Arkansas; March 16, 1943.)

Midori Oura

[Back in California] our junior high graduation day approached and we excitedly discussed credits, programs, and what to wear. At last the great day came. My name was called. I grasped my diploma and tripped across the stage. I saw my mother's beaming face. I remembered that Father was smiling and so were my two sisters, who had come down from college just to see me graduate.

Tanji Tashiko

In my childhood days, Mother used to scold me a lot for not obeying her. I don't blame her for scolding me so often because of the way I "acted up" on her quite a few times. She tells me to do something but I don't do it. That was my bad habit during my childhood. In the games, too. I liked to be the leader or the boss and didn't like someone else to be the leader and so that's how I got into trouble with someone else. When I grew older, I could remember back to how naughty I was, but I still am naughty.

Shagao Hamada

Another thing I'll never forget is when we had to part from my sister, who had to evacuate before us and we couldn't go with them because of not being ready to evacuate. I never felt so sad in all my life. Everybody in the family was crying. Next time I get out of here, first thing I'll do is to go see the little nephew of mine.

Multiple generations of the Furushiro family pose for a group portrait at Jerome.
Courtesy of the UALR Center for Arkansas History and Culture, Life Interrupted Collection

Notes

1. Jan Fielder Ziegler, *The Schooling of Japanese American Children at Relocation Centers During World War II: Miss Mabel Jamison and Her Teaching of Art at Rohwer, Arkansas* (Lewiston, NY: The Mellen Press, 2005), 126–27.

2. Excerpts from Diary of Evacuee, Rohwer Relocation Center, McGehee, Arkansas, Austin Smith Papers, MG04350, Arkansas History Commission, Little Rock, Arkansas.

3. Interview with Kazuko "Kaz" Fujishima, internee at Jerome Relocation Center in Arkansas, December 16, 2003. Center for Arkansas History and Culture, University of Arkansas at Little Rock, Life Interrupted Project.

Chapter 4
Voices: Life in the Camps—School Life and Activities

At the Rohwer camp, the school enrollment in 1943 was more than 2,000, with eighty-seven teachers (both white and Japanese). John A. Trice was the school superintendent. Jerome had a slightly greater number of both students and teachers, with Amon G. Thompson as the superintendent.[1]

Recruiting and keeping teachers in such trying conditions was difficult, despite the pay that was more than double what Arkansas teachers typically made. A bulletin for teachers written as the Rohwer schools got started lists the challenges faced by teachers at the camp:

> Our temporary quarters are neither beautiful nor extremely comfortable. Let us not dwell on these facts, but try to make each room as attractive as possible, through careful housekeeping. Pay close attention to ventilation, heat and light. The stoves in your room are very effective if you master the use of [their] draft controls.

> During wet weather we will have mud. Encourage the pupils to remove as much as possible before entering rooms. It will be nearly impossible to remove all of it.

> We will start school with very few texts, and in many instances with none. Each teacher will work out a program for her classes during this period....

> Each pupil is to provide his own paper, pencils, etc.[2]

While camp schools faced obstacles, nearby local school officials had complaints, too, protesting that the centers were taking away all their best teachers, leaving them understaffed. The camps were understaffed, too, because, despite the higher salary at the centers, many local teachers left due to dissatisfaction with the living conditions, shortage of supplies, and heavy responsibilities. Many no doubt had uncertainties and mixed feelings about the mission of the schools and how they would relate to the students. Those who stayed, however, often developed close relationships with their students. After a while, many of the teaching positions were filled by residents of the camps.

Elementary school class at Rohwer, working at makeshift desks; November 1942.
Courtesy of the Butler Center for Arkansas Studies, Edna A. Miller Collection

As one young woman internee who was pressed into service as a teacher wrote in her diary on February 13, 1943:

> Teaching is certainly fruitless when you have no textbooks or equipment to work with. You have to keep talking and illustrating. Office practice is rather a farce with no machinery—not even a typewriter. Students in my classes are disciplined, but B.'s class is a tower of Babel—don't see how he could get anything over with so many distractions and so much noise. Study hall groups are small but clannish—there is a lack of respect for teachers (which is so much a part of school under ordinary circumstances)...

> School rooms are so very dusty. They're terribly crowded, light is inadequate—no blinds and noise of band practicing is enough to drive a teacher to drink. Just found out there wasn't even a dictionary to be had at high school.[3]

The Japanese parents of the children in the camps—who held education in very high esteem—were concerned about how these schools would stack up next to the schools their children had attended back in California, and they worried how the situation might affect their children's academic futures, particularly if colleges did not accept credits earned at the camp schools.

As they settled in at their new schools, the young Japanese Americans proved themselves to be generally strong students who worked hard on their studies, finishing assignments and asking for more. There were very few problems with discipline. However, there were signs that the young people were not totally on board with their new environment. When the school at Rohwer opened, a student reportedly chalked "Jap Prison" on the tar-paper wall of the school room.[4] And the young woman internee who became a camp teacher wrote in her diary on April 7, 1943: "Hear a boy was expelled from school for insubordination. Students of Japanese extraction were rare problems in the matter of discipline back in California. The present situation has much to do with their cocky ways."[5]

The start of school life also allowed teens' social life to emerge. As historian Russell Bearden wrote: "With the beginning of school the Japanese students soon immersed themselves in the business of being teenagers. They organized school clubs and honor societies, elected school officers, scheduled sporting events between classes and between the two center schools, and published a school newspaper and annual."[6]

In their autobiographies, the students reminisced about their former school activities and hobbies in California, as well as expressing their hopes and fears—and frustrations—about their changed educational circumstances.

Grace Ige

My days at school [in California] were awfully busy and I often stayed after school because of all the activities. I am good in sewing, art, general science, and sports. Sewing is my best hobby. And, I love typing. I like to play basketball, baseball, and volleyball and do many other activities. I love to speak good English and I can understand it very good!

I like history because you know what the person is talking about. I love knowing about what's going on today as well as learning about things that happened a long time ago. Vacation is a wonderful thing. I never took a vacation unless you count going to Arkansas. It was the first time I'd left California.

Floyd Ouye

Naturally, the school [in Rohwer] came before my work, so from December 1st, 1942, I returned to my normal school life, hoping that some day I might be able to serve my country and defend the good old United States of America.

Roy Tanaka

My favorite studies are mathematics and science. I am majoring in Academic and plan to go to some vocational school or college. Now that we are in camp, my hopes are to get the most education I can get, and mental training. Since we have not been to school for almost half a year, we are probably left far behind the "outside" people, but my hopes are to catch up with the people outside. We started school about two months later than people outside, so my idea is to have two months of school during summer so we can catch up with the time.

In English, a subject which I do not care for very much, I hope the teacher will make it interesting so I would like English by the time I am promoted. In English, my favorites are short stories and novels.

Walking in Their Shoes
If you were held in a place like Rohwer or Jerome, what kinds of activities would you do to try to maintain a normal kind of life? Would you join the band or the newspaper staff? Would you play basketball or lift weights?

My hobbies are sports and stamps. I have participated in nearly all sports at my old school and made the team in most cases. My favorite sport is baseball. I can play any position coach puts me. My favorite positions are catcher, pitcher, and third base.

I have been enjoying camp life, but deep down in my heart lies anger towards this war. If there was no war, I always think we people of America would not have to be put into internment camps such as this one. The people of the outside world would not have to suffer under heavy taxes, priorities, rationing, and many other inconvenient laws if this was not happening....So ends my story, saying that, in camp, study is the best ammunition to take out to the outer world with you.

Frank Sakioka

Being fortunate to be able to go to school in this camp, I

64

Floyd Ouye
My interest is mostly with the Boy Scouts. I joined the Troop #91 in the latter part of November, 1938. This troop is under the leadership of Paul Shimada. As to date, I have learned many new ideas and the right steps to become a good citizen. "The Scout of today is the man of tomorrow." I am enjoying everything I do on hikes. The hikes were made possible by Robert Kishita, Cubmaster, who received permission from Captain Hastings to go out on hikes.

There was an active Boy Scout program for the boys in the camps in Arkansas. In August 1943, a five-day Boy Scout camp was held on the banks of the Mississippi River. Nearly a hundred boys from Rohwer and a few less from Jerome attended, together with a small troop from the nearby town of Arkansas City.

Poster drawn by Keyoze Toyofuku at Rohwer. *Courtesy of the Butler Center for Arkansas Studies*

Henry Hiroto
[Back in California] I was in the model airplane and boat-making club. Also in a social club, rather a skating club. I was sticking around with the school gang or group....I can play baseball, basketball, football, tennis, ping pong, volleyball, etc. Swimming is my favorite at all times, just no exercising bar. Fishing and hunting are my outside field sports.

My hobby is making model planes and boats. I also like to take apart motors and make things out of the parts.

Rohwer Résumé Yearbook; 1944.
Courtesy of the Butler Center for Arkansas Studies

Mary Sato (referring to herself as "she")
She enjoys the classes very much. Sometimes when some students act sort of sassy, she feels very sorry for the teacher

and wishes that the students would be more thoughtful towards the teacher. She thinks that it is very hard to teach a whole class of Japanese.

Minoru Takai

School has started but right now it isn't like the schools I used to go to in California. The school in California had nice comfortable desks, all kinds of shops, but print shop was my favorite shop, good assemblies and all kinds of sports to see.

Well, those days are memories now. Rohwer is permanent and school has started. Right now its buildings don't look like school buildings yet. But in due time I think we'll see some changes made. I'm looking forward to that time....Right now I have American literature and I will try to pass with at least a grade better than C.

Pearl Bristow teaches a ninth-grade class at Rohwer High School.
Courtesy of the UALR Center for Arkansas History and Culture, Life Interrupted Collection; original held by the National Archives and Records Administration

Yas Miyao

I have taken up physics in school (Rohwer H.S.) and found it to be interesting. But either I am ignorant to understand the assignments, or Mr. Cook believes us to be so smart that he teaches in much progress and advance. I do not know. I really hope to know physics much more better than what I little know of it and accomplish it....I entered Rohwer High School resolving to accomplish every effort I have failed. It is tough, but I'll fight on to gain the approbation of all.

High school study hall in the mess hall at Rohwer.
Courtesy of the Butler Center for Arkansas Studies, Edna A. Miller Collection

LEFT· GRIEVANCES
OF BOY'S AND GIRL'S
WEEK ARE BURIED
AS THE HATCHET.

Rohwer Résumé Yearbook; 1944.
Courtesy of the Butler Center for Arkansas Studies, Rosalie Santine Gould–Mabel Jamison Vogel Collection

Ando Yoshimi

I don't know if it's my mind that won't work, but I can't keep my mind on any kind of work or study. I feel as if everything is running up and down my whole body, from head to toe.

From the diary of a young woman held at the Rohwer camp, November 13, 1942[7]:

Schools have started. Quite a few evacuee teachers, Caucasians supervising. Children having a grand time imitating the southern drawl.

Grace Okumura

At present, I'm attending the Rohwer Senior High School as a low junior. Something tells me I will graduate from this school whether I like it or not. I hope I'll get what I want in this school.

What worries me is that I hear rumors that this school has a very low standard of teaching. I hope it isn't true because otherwise we won't be worth anything after we graduate.

Jane Sakata

I'll never forget the old days in the Stockton High School [back in California]. At the present I'm looking forward to this Rohwer High School too.

These pages of the Résumé Yearbook at Rohwer, 1945, seem to be especially revealing.

In addition to school work, students took part in many activities, including art, music, yearbook, newspaper, drama, sports, and clubs.

As with any high school, the yearbooks from this time tell a lot but leave a lot of things a mystery, too. All the back stories and inside jokes shared among these students will remain theirs alone, but the yearbooks do give a glimpse into camp life for these teenagers. Especially intriguing is the "burying of the hatchet" between the boys and girls.

The Denson High School Band practices outside at Jerome Relocation Center. Sam Mibu is in the center row with a French horn.
Courtesy of the UALR Center for Arkansas History and Culture, Life Interrupted Collection

All graduates, even those in extraordinary circumstances, adopt a reflective mood as their schooling ends. The following reminiscence, written by editorial writer Yoshikazu Sakakura for the 1945 Résumé Yearbook, is especially touching, as he and his classmates face an uncertain post-war future.[8]

Reminiscence

Since the opening of the Rohwer Senior High School in October of 1942, we have made great advances in establishing as normal a school as humanly possible. We now have a school constitution, a student government, a chapter of the National Honor Society, a student paper, numerous active clubs, and an auditorium—a far cry from the day when we first faced the bleak barrack school rooms with a shortage of teachers. In short, we have established Rohwer Hi as a semblance of a normal high school. It is a record which we may well be proud of.

But the forward progress must go on. By January of the next year, this center will have closed; this semester will mark the finale of the brief but outstanding history of Rohwer High School. What will that mean to us? Of course it will mean the end of slogging through mud to school, bare school rooms, and other unpleasant conditions connected with a center school; but it will also mean the end of intimate companionships, close friendships—all those beautiful things one normally associates with a high school.

Courtesy of the Butler Center for Arkansas Studies, Rosalie Santine Gould–Mabel Jamison Vogel Collection

After the years have rolled away and the sands of life run down the hourglass of time, we will look back with nostalgic tears, lumps in our throats, and pangs in our breasts toward Rohwer—the place where we have enjoyed the greatest gift of God, friendship—with tender emotions not possible to be felt now. Our lives have hardly been beds of roses. The ever-present insects, the mud, the penetrating cold have made life miserable for those of us laboring over books. Many were the times when we wished to desist from our labors and declare ourselves free; yet we plugged on and though labor was very painful, the fruits will ripen and yield a rich harvest—a fuller and happier life.

And now like the mighty sun setting in his halo of beauty, glory, and grandeur, the Rohwer High School has come to the end of its appointed time—gone, yes; but never to be forgotten. With many a fond backward glance toward Rohwer with its joy and gloom, its love and hate, its laughter and tears, and its bleakness and beauty, we will start climbing the ever-ascending trail to a brighter and more glorious tomorrow!

Fashion Drawings

High fashion seems strange with the bleak surroundings of the Rohwer internment camp, but fashion drawing was popular, especially with teenage girls and young women of the camp. These drawings (the evening gown drawing created by Wilma Matsubara and the woman in a green dress drawn by an unknown artist) reflect some of the most significant shifts in fashion during that time period. The dropped waist and short skirt of the 1920s through mid-1930s gave way to a more natural waistline and longer length in the 1940s. Movie stars such as Joan Crawford helped popularize the broad-shouldered look in both day and evening wear.

(Source: *The Art of Living: Japanese American Creative Experience at Rohwer,* Butler Center for Arkansas Studies)

Notes

1. Russell Bearden, "Life Inside Arkansas's Japanese-American Relocation Centers." *Arkansas Historical Quarterly* 48 (Summer 1989): 188.

2. "Bulletin for Teachers," ca. late 1942. Rosalie Santine Gould–Mabel Jamison Vogel Collection, Butler Center for Arkansas Studies, Central Arkansas Library System, Little Rock, Arkansas.

3. Excerpts from Diary of Evacuee, Rohwer Relocation Center, McGehee, Arkansas, Austin Smith Papers, MG04350, Arkansas History Commission, Little Rock, Arkansas.

4. Lane Ryo Hirabayashi, "The Impact of Incarceration on the Education of Nisei Schoolchildren," in *Japanese Americans: From Relocation to Redress*, ed. Roger Daniels, Sandra C. Taylor, and Harry H. L. Kitano (Salt Lake City: University of Utah Press, 1986), 48.

5. Excerpts from Diary of Evacuee, Rohwer Relocation Center.

6. Bearden, "Life Inside," 188.

7. Excerpts from Diary of Evacuee, Rohwer Relocation Center.

8. Résumé Yearbook at Rohwer, 1945, Rosalie Santine Gould–Mabel Jamison Vogel Collection.

The Japanese American teens in the camps were no different from teens everywhere in their high level of social activity, with friends and sometimes with romantic interests. And they found plenty of time and opportunity for socializing in the camps. They were all in the same situation—in camp for the foreseeable future and uncertain what the future beyond their sight would be. In the meantime, they went to school, they hung out, they daydreamed, and they flirted.

Historian Russell Bearden characterized the social aspects of the "business of being teenagers" in the camps this way:

> Within time friendships were formed, pecking orders established, and romances began to bloom. Once again young men could become, in the lexicon of center slang, "dame dazed" for the most attractive "slick chicks" and "ready Hedys" in camp, and young ladies could reject those panting "dog faces" or "void coupons" and instead swoon for "hunks-of-heartbreak" and the best "pepper shakers" at center dances. If a young man were lucky and the young girl's Issei parents were not "crab-patched curfew keepers" he might be able to swing a "smooch date" with his favorite girl beneath the warm shadows of the block barracks.[1]

Clara Haegawa and Tad Mijake looking out from a guard tower at Jerome Relocation Center.
Courtesy of the UALR Center for Arkansas History and Culture, Life Interrupted Collection

More than 2,000 marriages took place in the ten relocation centers around the country. Jerome recorded 103 and Rohwer 153; no one got divorced in the Arkansas centers.[2]

Some see a darker side of the hyper-social teenage behavior in the camps, however. Unmoored from their previous lives as members of a fully functioning family household, teens in the camps sometimes acted in ways that mirrored behavior in other situations of imprisonment. A community analysis report filed with the War Relocation Authority about the Jerome camp said that the incarceration of Japanese American youth had the following effects:

> Some of the trends among the Nisei youth are racial hypersensitivity coupled with a disparagement of other races (Jews, [blacks], Mexicans, White trash [*sic*]); gangs have formed since it gives its members a sense of power, exclusiveness, and defiance motivated by an individual insecurity in the larger configuration of world events. Then too, the uncertainty of the future is compensated by living merely in the present; thus, recreation activities are overemphasized. As could be expected ambition has been watered in many cases, and a concern with the obvious and superficial (clothes, ability to dance, etc.) exists.[3]

It is hard to say, though, how much of a part incarceration played in this behavior and how much is typical of teens in general, particularly teens with a lot of time on their hands and waning parental control. Too, the common racial attitudes of the time (before the civil rights movement and the desegregation of American schools in the 1950s and 1960s) were not particularly enlightened, so the same types of racial scorn would be commonplace in the greater Arkansas community.

As the Rohwer students' autobiographies show, like many other aspects of young people's lives during this time, friendships were often disrupted during the evacuation—both friendships from back home in California and those that developed in the assembly centers after evacuation. It is clear that many evacuees dearly missed their friends back on the West Coast—Japanese American, white, or another group—as well as friends who had been sent to other camps. They even had to leave their pets behind.

Walking in Their Shoes

What would it be like to be separated from your friends by what seems to be an arbitrary and unfair process? For example, at school, look around at your classmates and choose something that you can group people by: the length of their hair, whether they are wearing shoes with laces, if they are wearing pants or shorts. Now, think about what it would be like to be sent away—or see your friends sent away—for having lace-up shoes. Of course, the situation faced by these young people was more complicated than that, but their separation and exclusion from their friends in California seemed just as unfair.

Mary Kobayashi

I miss my friends from home. We always enjoyed a good laugh and, well, they were just a swell bunch of girls. We had our bad moments, such as bickering and even quarreling among ourselves, but everyone was so jovial it was forgotten in a minute. I could describe each and every one but it will have to wait until some other time. Parting from them when evacuation arose was one of the hardest and saddest things that ever happened to me.

Masao Kadokura

When we evacuated from Los Angeles to Santa Anita I didn't feel like I do now. I thought it would be like taking a vacation. But when I boarded the bus to Santa Anita I did not feel so good. I felt as though I was departing from everything, and an empty, sick feeling entered my stomach. I felt as though I would never see my friends again. After the bus left and we were halfway to Santa Anita, the empty feeling left me, and I began wondering how camp life would be—who would be there, what friends I would make, etc. As we entered Santa Anita the people already there stared at us as though we were on exhibition. On the following day another group was supposed to come in from where I was evacuated. However, when I heard that part of that group went to Manzanar [another internment camp, in California] I was disappointed very much because my very best friend was supposed to have come in that day. I was so disappointed I couldn't eat for two days. I felt very lonely until the day that he wrote to me. This friend of mine is an old acquaintance from the days I used to live in Seattle. He was almost my twin—he was born on the same day, same month, same year, same city, same state, and the same block. He and his family also moved to Los Angeles soon after we moved there. We still write each other by mail, but I don't think I will ever forget how I felt when I heard that he had gone to another center. That same sick feeling came over me when we left Santa Anita for this camp.

Closing of the Jerome Relocation Center. One of the farewell dances held the evening before departure of residents to other centers. It was humid at Jerome and the young couple at the door went out for fresh air; June 14, 1944.
Photo by Hikaru Iwasaki; courtesy of the National Archives and Records Administration, Records of the War Relocation Authority, 1941–1989

Tsutoma Ihara

I miss my pet rabbit Ango and her litters. I have raised about thirty rabbits. Because of the evacuation, I had to sell my rabbit. I gave my Ango to my friend to take care of. She was a beautiful rare type of Angora.

Satoshi Oishi

Even though I knew how good California was I never realized how much better it was until I left it. After staying at Santa Anita for approximately six months the relocation began. Every train that left also left behind broken families, lonely boys, and heartsick girls.

Teenagers pose together at Jerome Relocation Center. Left to right: Jackie Kobara, a native Louisianan visiting Jerome; Jim Okura; Susuna "Babe" Okura (later killed in action in France, 1944); Sam Ozaki; and Harry "Dumbo" Oda.
Courtesy of the UALR Center for Arkansas History and Culture, Life Interrupted Collection

George Kimura

In my seventh and eighth grade [in California], Eugene Dahm and Gordon Standlund were my best friends. They were well bred and mannered. In

RIGHT · THREE BOOKWORMS ARE CAUGHT AT THEIR, USUAL PASTIME.

Rohwer Résumé Yearbook; 1944.
Courtesy of the Butler Center for Arkansas Studies, Rosalie Santine Gould–Mabel Jamison Vogel Collection

class, we were called the three musketeers. We were usually ahead of the class work and frequently in plays together. We became very interested in radio and decided to make radio sets so we could communicate with each other.

In the ninth grade, Eugene and I took up aviation. We were now thirteen....In my sophomore year, I majored in auto mechanics. This course included aviation. During the schooltime, Eugene and I started to construct an airplane with the assistance of our shop teacher. We had spent months designing it. In class, the shop teacher made me his assistant school teacher. I received straight A's in that course....Most of the Japanese down here are very smart. There were only about fifty Japanese students in this school....

Three teenagers walk down a dirt road at Rohwer.
Courtesy of the UALR Center for Arkansas History and Culture, Life Interrupted Collection

During Saturdays, I had to go to a Japanese school. My school work kept me very busy, yet I had time to play with Eugene and Gordon. Usually we played tennis but we were experimenting and building airplanes most of the time. I went to some movies, which was mostly aviation films.

1941, a dark year of my life, changed things. Father became ill, my little brother got hurt in an accident, we had moved to Los Angeles. Eugene and I were just about finishing our airplane but we had to leave it and also I had left all my friends. The boys in Los Angeles are very noisy and vulgar, which makes me sick.

September, 1941, Father passed away, my grief was heavy. December 7, 1941, brought war which I knew would come. Evacuation came. I wondered of our future and our new home. I was angry, dazed, and gloomy. Santa Anita, not such a bad place, except a little crowded and the stables smelled bad. I took up a hobby of model plane building. Most of the boys here are not like my old friends, they laugh over nothing too much, oh well, laughing brightens up the dull camp.

Now came Rohwer, here, I have no hobby, and lost interest in aviation. I am a Buddhist and don't care for social gatherings. I am <u>totally</u> sick of being in camp, and mostly of the boys here. Most of them joke around too much, they are very vulgar, noisy, and make too many silly cracks. During the year 1941, I missed a school year, lost interest in studying. Grief, anger and wondering caused me to forget most of the things I learned. I recall the days when the teachers told me I was very bright and was active in school work, but in this school, I am very dull and very inactive....My brother is now news editor of the Rohwer Outpost....I have enough experience to fly an airplane, construct and repair gasoline and electrical engines, construct and repair radio sets. My accomplishment in camp is worthless. I pray to God to end the war quick so I can get out of this hell quick.

A group of teenagers, including Susuna Okura and Eso Masuda, poses in front of barracks at Jerome.
Courtesy of the UALR Center for Arkansas History and Culture, Life Interrupted Collection

I say to Eugene and Gordon, till we meet again, and I'm sure we will someday, when we succeed. Finis.

Janet Sato

During my six years of grade school, I have made many friends of all nationalities. We have all worked together harmoniously and we have carried our friendship through Junior High School and Senior High. We have enjoyed football games, parties, socials and such that when it came time for me to depart for the evacuation, it seemed like I was losing all the warm friendships that I have shared with my Caucasian friends....Ever since war was declared, the lives of us American-Japanese have been days of uncertainty. We couldn't put our whole hearted souls into our studies....On October the fourth we left Santa Anita for Rohwer, Arkansas. We find Rohwer to be the same as California when it comes to weather but something does lack and that is the friendship of these Caucasian people.

74

Frank Shimazaki

When war broke out I was very startled that Japan would do such a thing. The very next day my dad and sister lost their jobs. We were all worried. When the evacuation program was introduced we were more worried. Our Caucasian friends offered to help us. They even brought us boxes of canned goods....We started to sell our furniture. We heard of many people getting gypped but it didn't happen to us. We spent a lot of money on buying new clothes. We were evacuated on the 7th of May to Santa Anita Assembly Center. The very next day I explored the whole camp. I felt funny eating in mess halls but I got used to it. After 5 months I had made many new friends. We had to part and go to different relocation centers. My best friends went to Wyoming. I can still picture my friends on that train waving as the train started to move. That is a sight I will never forget and I hope someday when the war will end that we will meet again not as boys but as full-grown men.

Tazuko Inauye

If it were not for the evacuation, I don't believe I would know fifty percent of the people I know now. Practically every day I meet someone new. Also it is very interesting to hear the stories of other places and assembly centers. One thing I regret is the fact that they separated some people to other centers. Although I correspond with them, that will not fully make up for the fun I would be having with them if they were here. As a whole, though, this center has most of the people I know. In all my life I never thought that I would be coming to Arkansas. Although I like it here, no matter what happens, I hope they will send us back to [the town of] Stockton where I spent my life till now—where I could really call home.

June Yamanaka

Every week we get letters from our American friends at home who write to us telling us that they miss us and hope that the war will end soon so we can go back to the old ways of living. I, too, am hoping the same things.

Shagao Hamada

When we left Santa Anita, it was also a sad moment. I'd met many new friends and now had to part with them. And just when I'd met a swell gal, too. I'll never forget her. I always receive a couple of letters weekly from her.

While the young people missed their old friends from home and from the

RIGHT • WHAT GOES ON?

Rohwer Résumé Yearbook; 1944.
Courtesy of the Butler Center for Arkansas Studies, Rosalie Santine Gould–Mabel Jamison Vogel Collection

assembly centers, many new friendships formed in the camps, too. Some people made friends more easily than others, though.

Buck Sakurai

The evacuation has been a great benefit as well as a bad effect. When I came into camp in Santa Anita I did not know very many people. Then I played baseball with a group of boys and then we went around as a gang with them and I became more of a, what people called, "rugged boy." This is one change camp life has made me do but the other is good. It has changed me from a shy boy to more of a talkative boy although I am still a little shy. Also in camp life it has given me more of a chance to play whereas if I were back home I would be working all the time.

Yashike Kadama

I guess my childhood feeling is still inside of me—that I mean the way I feel about things never changes. Nowadays, too. I'm always sad because I don't have a friend to trust. I don't have anybody to talk over things. I try to make friends but it seems to me they're not my friend. I talk with them but they don't speak the same language. That I mean I think the other way and she thinks another way. We never seem to talk the same things. I eat alone and do everything alone. Gee, sometimes you can't stand being alone. Every time you feel as if you might go crazy, but just the same, I take it.

Mineko Shiroishi

We were relocated to Rohwer Relocation Center on October 6, 1942. The friends whom I met at Santa Anita are now scattered in relocation centers throughout the United States. I have few friends with whom I am intimately acquainted in this center at present, but since the opportunities for friendship here are endless, I am quite sure *that I will be able to adapt myself socially very quickly.*

Unidentified author

And, the latest [club] in Rohwer is called "Arky-teens," with about 18 or 20 girls. I have not been in the club long enough to give my opinion about it....Now, about crowds or gangs. I like to mingle with people, but I don't approve of groups going around in a bunch of more than 2 or 3 girls at a time.

Japanese American soldiers of the 442nd Combat Team at a dance at Camp Shelby in Mississippi. Young Japanese American women from Jerome and Rohwer Relocation Centers in Arkansas traveled there to keep them company; June 1943.
Courtesy of the Library of Congress Prints and Photographs Division

Unsurprisingly, these young people did not write a lot about dating or romance in these autobiographies, which were a school assignment, but, to be sure, these teens were like any others—developing crushes, dabbling in romances, and suffering heartbreaks.

Kimiko Oshiro

All my girl friends started to talk about this boy and that boy. I got kind of interested in them too but I never talked about them in front of girls because they will tease me, so I just kept it to myself.

A young woman internee who taught school at Rohwer had this to say about some romancing she observed (note that the people from the Santa Anita and Stockton assembly centers are still identifying with these groups): "Little Neebo dance for ex-Santa Anitans and a Li'l Pancho dance for Stocktonians....Jitterbugging was the thing. Dances in center are too dark and older chaperones should be present. Witnessed first-class necking scene across the way. Fast going for first-time daters."[4]

More than the school writing assignments, the yearbooks produced by the students of the high schools of both Rohwer and Jerome give insight into the social lives of the students. They look much like yearbooks anywhere in America—full of smiling faces, raucous activities, and private jokes.

In the private-joke realm, it's hard to beat the tradition of "willing" certain things to friends in the pages of a yearbook. Most are light-hearted and humorous (though we don't always know exactly why), but the war creeps in, too—as always. Here are some selections from the "Where There's a Will—There's a Way" section of Rohwer Winter Hi-Lites Yearbook from winter 1942–43:

I, Tomiko Shibata, will my A's in Civics to the dumbest person in the Senior B class next to "Wildcat."

I, Mary Nakao, will my masculine voice to George Yamasaki.

I, Sue Teranishi, will my title of having a white complexion to Kaz Hirata.

I, Haruko Matsushita, will my ability to play Chopin to Ben Boogie, an incoming sophomore.

I, Fumiko "Webster" Oshita, will my extensive vocabulary to Hank "Grapes of Wrath" Okano.

I, Dick "Dead-Eye" Shimasaki, will my ability to sink them to the U.S. Navy.

I, Yukio Ikegami, leave my curls to the little wet ducks. He's all wet too—(holy smoke can't you take a joke?)

I, Akemi Terashita, leave my glamorous coiffure and dramatic coat to anyone who wants to stun the stag line.

Rohwer Résume Yearbook; 1945.
*Courtesy of the Butler Center for Arkansas Studies,
Rosalie Santine Gould–Mabel Jamison Vogel Collection*

I, Sachi Masaki, leave my football legs to Miss Shiz Eya.

We, Yoshikatsu Takada, Noboru Sakakura, George Umeda, Hidoo Nakagawa, Hideo Okumeto, will our quietness to Ray Kurihara. It takes the quietness of five people to balance his noise.

I, Mildred Ikezoe, contribute my machine gun (chatter) to the war effort.

Notes

1. Russell Bearden, "Life Inside Arkansas's Japanese-American Relocation Centers." *Arkansas Historical Quarterly* 48 (Summer 1989): 191.
2. Bearden, "Life Inside," 191.
3. Kayoshi Hamanaka, "Problems of the Evacuees," Jerome Relocation Center, February 16, 1943, WRA Community Analysis Section, Record Group 1342, National Archives, quoted in Jan Fielder Ziegler, *The Schooling of Japanese American Children at Relocation Centers During World War II: Miss Mabel Jamison and Her Teaching of Art at Rohwer, Arkansas* (Lewiston, NY: The Mellen Press, 2005).
4. Excerpts from Diary of Evacuee, Rohwer Relocation Center, McGehee, Arkansas, Austin Smith Papers, MG04350, Arkansas History Commission, Little Rock, Arkansas.

Chapter 6
Voices: Finding a New Home after the Closing of the Camps

On December 17, 1944, President Franklin D. Roosevelt signed Public Proclamation No. 21, marking the end of the exclusion order that had kept Japanese Americans from their homes on the West Coast. This followed the court case of Mitsuye Endo, who was held at the high-security center at Tule Lake. The U.S. Supreme Court heard the case in October 1944, and the ruling in Endo's favor, finding that detention of Japanese Americans in relocation centers was unconstitutional and racist, was announced on December 18. This was the only case that had been decided in favor of a Japanese American plaintiff.[1]

Many of the young Nisei men and women in the camps had already been resettled by the time Jerome closed on June 30, 1944. Residents were then moved to other camps, including far-away Gila River in Arizona and nearby Rohwer. World War II in Asia officially ended with the formal surrender of Japan in September 1945. The United States had dropped two atomic bombs on Japan the month before—first on Hiroshima, then on Nagasaki—hastening the end of the war. The war in Europe had ended in the spring with the fall of Nazi Germany.

After it closed as an internment camp, the facilities at Jerome were used as a prisoner-of-war camp for Germans until the end of the war in Europe. Rohwer closed on November 30, 1945.

After the camps closed, a few families stayed in Arkansas for a time, though almost all had left within a year, as people of Japanese descent were prohibited from owning land in Arkansas. On February 13, 1943, the Arkansas state legislature had passed the Alien Land Act, barring any Japanese citizen or alien from buying or owning land in the state. This was later ruled unconstitutional.[2]

In an editorial titled "Democracy at Home" published in the twice-weekly *Rohwer Outpost*, the writer responded to the actions of the Arkansas legislature this way: "In the final analysis, very

Resettlement

At first, the War Relocation Authority (WRA) used the term **resettlement** to describe the movement of so-called loyal Japanese immigrants and Japanese Americans out of the camps during World War II. Today, the term is used more generally to encompass the movements of those with Japanese ancestry both during and following the war.

Not long after the camps opened, some Japanese Americans were already being allowed to leave the camps to attend college or to provide seasonal farm labor (as there was much demand for labor during the war). Many people, especially young people, took advantage of these opportunities, even though they faced discrimination (and sometimes violence), difficulty in finding housing, separation from their friends and families, and a lack of anything but unskilled jobs.

A more comprehensive resettlement policy followed to get "loyal" Japanese Americans out of the camps. The WRA viewed the camps as an opportunity to scatter Japanese Americans around the country and end the prewar Japanese enclaves on the West Coast, integrating Japanese Americans into white mainstream society. It also feared that, without such a resettlement program, the people in the camps would become permanently dependent on the government. Ironically, the idea of "loyal" Japanese Americans

(Continued next page)

few if any of the persons of Japanese ancestry have had any intention of staying in the boundaries of this state after the war, so it appears that the legislative representatives of Arkansas should reconsider their decision. Is it worth going against the fundamental tenets of the U.S. Constitution in order to satisfy the unsubstantiated fears of agricultural competition from fellow Americans who have no intention of staying in this state?"[3] Regarding this, historian Jan Ziegler noted:

> This final twist in the *Outpost*—the editor's invocation of the Constitution—clearly served to further underscore the absurdity of the schools' intention to teach the "tenets of Democracy" to the Nisei students. Thus the complexities and perplexities of the situation—the gaping disconnect between the publicly-proclaimed intentions and privately perceived realities—became apparent: The schools were expected to "Americanize" the sons and daughters of men and women deemed incapable of—and disallowed from—ever becoming American, and to do so to a captive populace abruptly and unconstitutionally impounded out of the very society which these young people were to be taught to embrace, and which, in point of fact, they already *did* embrace....Before these young Nisei were uprooted by their government, theirs was a world where, often, their best buddies were Caucasian peers. It was a world of American movies and American radio programs; a world of American books and American activities.[4]

Arkansas governor Homer Adkins was reluctant to allow Japanese Americans to attend college at schools in the state, fearing this would contribute to the integration of higher education in Arkansas (until the late 1950s, African Americans and whites attended separate schools). All Arkansas colleges turned away Japanese Americans except for what is now the University of the Ozarks in Clarksville in Johnson County, which allowed one Nisei young man to enroll in the autumn of 1945, as the war was ending.[5]

being allowed to leave camp seemed to go against the very idea behind the mass removal, which was based on racist presumptions that anyone of Japanese ancestry posed a threat to the nation. As historian Roger Daniels wrote in his book *Prisoners Without Trial,* "only after mass evacuation and incarceration had appeased the public and the politicians was the executive branch ready to assess the loyalty of the Japanese Americans."

Those considered loyal remained in camp or left for resettlement or military service, while those found to be disloyal were segregated into higher-security camps through the end of the war and, in some cases, after the war.

To be resettled outside, Japanese Americans had to secure a sponsor, show proof of employment or education, and submit to FBI background checks.

The WRA put out a propaganda campaign, with representatives touring the camps and making presentations about resettlement. Materials circulated both inside and outside the camps showing resettlers happily integrated into society. These images attempted to show the public that Japanese Americans could blend into white middle-class society. In keeping with its policies of assimilation, the WRA also told people leaving camp to maintain a low profile, speak only English, and stay away from other Japanese Americans.

(Source: Densho Encyclopedia, "Resettlement")

Some, although generally the older internees suffering from the normal ailments of age, never got to leave the camps at all. A total of 244 people died in the Arkansas camps: 168 at Rohwer and 76 at Jerome. While many of the

Buddhist families had their loved ones cremated, others were buried. The Rohwer cemetery has twenty-five graves that remain there today.[6]

The government eventually provided some restitution to Japanese Americans relocated during the war and their families. In 1948, the Evacuation Claims Act was passed, which gave some financial compensation, but it was very little compared to the actual worth of what people lost when they had to flee their homes. In the 1970s, a redress movement began to grow, driven primarily by the efforts of third-generation Sansei Japanese Americans to educate people about what had happened to their parents and grandparents during the war.

In 1983, the Commission on Wartime Relocation (established by Congress in 1980 to research what had led to the internment process) published a report critical of Executive Order 9066. It said, "Widespread ignorance of Japanese Americans contributed to a policy conceived in haste and executed in an atmosphere of fear and anger at Japan. A grave injustice was done."[7] The report recommended a congressional apology and financial compensation for living internees. It was not until 1988, however, that President Ronald Reagan made this a reality, saying, "Yes, the nation was then at war, struggling for its survival—and it's not for us to pass judgment upon those who may have made mistakes while engaged in that great struggle. Yet we must recognize that the internment of Japanese Americans was just that—a mistake. For throughout the war, Japanese Americans in the tens of thousands remained utterly loyal to the United States."[8]

At the closing of the Jerome Relocation Center, passengers for the train to the Gila River Relocation Center in Arizona leave the trucks and approach the train cars to which they have been assigned.
Courtesy of the UALR Center for Arkansas History and Culture, Life Interrupted Collection; original held by the National Archives and Records Administration

Payments of $20,000 were sent to former internees starting in 1990 and going for nearly a decade. A total of 82,250 people received more than $1.6 billion from the U.S. government's Office of Redress Administration.[9]

This was all still far in the future for the young people in the Arkansas camps, facing only uncertainty about what lay before them when they left the camps. Even at the start of their time in Arkansas, however, many students at Rohwer expressed their plans for their future (as well as their uncertainty about how they would now realize those plans) in the autobiographies they wrote in English class in 1942.

Nobuo Tomito

My future is to be an artist. I've liked drawing ever since I was in the fifth grade. I received nothing but "A's" and "B's" in my grammar school years.

When I started junior year, art became my chief interest. The first year I really learned a lot and I had lots of fun.

In the eighth grade, things started to come toward my life. I entered the Poppy Poster Contest, which was sponsored by the American Legion Dep't. Post 272. I took first place and received an American Legion (for excellence in Poppy) medal. I won again the next year and was I glad! I'm going to keep the two medals as long as I live! I was going to enter the contest again in the tenth grade but evacuation spoiled everything.

I was planning to go to an art institute after I get out of high school but the war affects all my plans. But, I'm looking forward to a future after the war.

Chitoshi Ryuto

Future life is doubtful to explain, but I'd like to continue my education as I can. For my future occupation, I'd like to be a diesel engineer, hope to be an aeronautical draftsman, wish to be an optometrist or an Army man.

Grace Okumura

After I graduate from Senior High School I'm planning to do some kind of stenographic work. How successful I'll be, I do not know. I think that it all depends as to how I go about in school on that line of work. I hope I won't lose my confidence so wish me luck!

A boy stands in front of graves at Rohwer Relocation Center; July 1943.
Courtesy of the UALR Center for Arkansas History and Culture, Life Interrupted Collection; original held by the National Archives and Records Administration

Emiko Taguchi

I don't have very much to say about evacuation, but I shall express myself in how I felt to leave the city in which I was born and raised [in California]. I just thought I was leaving piles of gold back there, and if the war should end, I thought I would like to go to my hometown to see the piles of gold again.

I guess most people in this camp are men and women

without houses after the war. This question I have been thinking about and am still thinking about it, too.

Tom Saito

I do not like to write about the future because I wrote about myself and the future to my English teacher back in 1940 when I entered high school. What I wrote did not come out the way I said it would. This time I will play smart and not write about the future but I hope this time it comes out a little better than that of the last time. I hate to waste paper like this but I think this is good enough.

George Kobayashi

Since the war has spoiled my chances as a reporter outside, I hope to study to the best of my ability so I can have my chance (in this free country) when I will be able to be free.

Thoughts of a seventeen-year-old boy after evacuation in 1942:

Before December 7, 1941, I had many plans for the future, but as war continued and hatred developed in the hearts of other Americans toward the Japanese Americans, I found that the life ahead was not going to be easy. Then came the evacuation. After remaining in the small over-populated assembly center and associating with the many different types of people every day, I became a completely changed person both physically and mentally.

These many changes have for the most part made me stronger, more determined, and alert to this fast-changing world. My camp barbell training has done everything for me, both for the muscles and for my mind. I now have the strength equal to that of two normal persons of my age, and in mind I have developed a firm, grim determination to do and complete to the best of my ability everything I undertake. It has taught me to remain calm and to keep a tranquil mind at all times.

I have also strengthened myself by observing those who yield to things that are wrong. I have seen those who will throw away their future because of this unfortunate incident (evacuation); and those who have the "Aw, what's the use" attitude. I have...learned that those who give up hope are giving up their only life.

Thus I have gained a strong mind and body through being placed in a center, which I am sure I would not have got if I had not been taken from my quiet home.

My plans are to relocate immediately upon graduation and

*get a good job until I am called for the army; there I will serve
to the best of my ability.*

*I HAVE NO PLANS FOR LIVING in the new post-war world,
but I will save as much money as possible for those who will
live in that world.*

**Note attached [probably written by Rohwer art teacher
Jamie Vogel]:** *This boy has relocated to Chicago, has a good
job, and is just waiting until Uncle Sam calls HIS time to go.
He says he KNOWS he will NOT come back from the war. But
he has had the satisfaction of working for a few short months
to make a few more things possible for the parents and little
sister he is leaving.*

Jim Tanaka

*Like thousands of American citizens of Japanese ancestry
that were interned in various relocation camps through the
great West "due to necessary measures of war," my future
is as yet quite uncertain and unpredictable, but, of this, I
am sure. The powers of terrorism and requests of peaceful
countries must be rushed and peace and rights of free people
restored once more.*

*All of us, young and old, are making many bitter sacrifices,
but I think we shall have to make more and more to end this
greatest war in the history of mankind.*

*I look forward to the future when all this shall be but a
memory and I can live in the most powerful and democratic
nation in the world, champion of peaceful and freedom-loving
people, regardless of race, color, or creed.*

This boy from a farming family put a positive spin on the internment experience,
feeling that he learned things he could apply later in his hoped-for life of farming:

Minoru Tsutsui

*The experience I have gotten from the evacuation is very
great. I always wanted to see something of the farming
towards the South lands and I got a chance. I also found out
how vast this great country really is. I hope that after the war I
will be able to go back to my sunny home in...the San Joaquin
Valley.*

As they faced the reality of leaving the camps, the young people in Arkansas
expressed an understandable mix of emotions, coupled with vast uncertainty.
The following are excerpts from post-evacuation plans written for a school
assignment in 1944.[10]

From a fifteen-year-old girl:

As I was coming down the walk toward our barrack unit Mom was returning from the laundry room with a kettle of hot water. As we neared each other I thought she looked very happy and thrilled at something. She suddenly whispered to me three words and kept on toward the barrack as though in a trance. Those three little words were unbelievable and miraculous; I stood there and stared straight into nothing. The "message" sent something tingling up and down my spine, right hand to left. The message was—"California is open!"

From a sixteen-year-old boy:

As I sat comfortably on a chair near the nice warm G.I. stove, I thought, "Gee! We're lucky that we could sit in a warm room and think what we want to be and do in the future while people out in London and other places where bombs continue to fall, wrecking their homes, do not know if they will be alive or dead in the next few seconds.

When I was walking to the shower I looked up into the sky thinking how lucky we are that stars up above are stars, and not enemy planes.

From a seventeen-year-old boy:

Would the people greet us [after the war] and say how they felt about the evacuation, or would they like our blood to leak from our body? Who knows these answers? No one will until somebody is brave enough to try it.

There is always one thing that bothers me. In the Constitution of the United States it says that there cannot be a mass evacuation of any racial group. Congress has changed this. If Congress has the right to change a constitution, why? Why does the United States have a constitution?

Henry Okamora (or Okamura)
WHAT I THINK OF GOING BACK TO CALIFORNIA:

I don't care if I go back or not, for we didn't have a ranch. All I care is that we get our furniture, such as refrigerator, radios, bureau, bicycle, toolbox, phonograph records, etc....

If I do go back what will I do? There's lots of other places where I could go instead of California, such as Michigan where our dearest friends are.

Oh, yes, I would like to go back to California and see our old classmates again (if they like to see me) and the teachers...but I know I will have a funny feeling inside me that will make me want to go elsewhere....I want to start my life all over in another state instead of just staying and thinking that California is the only state in the United States. In a way like this you will get so-called NARROW MINDED. We are supposed to broaden our mind instead of narrowing it.

Katsumi Sugimoto

My greatest ambition is farming. I have chosen farming because I know more about it than anything else. I have decided to follow the footsteps of my ancestors and continue farming. Another great ambition of mine is to die for my country if necessary. This can be done only when Americans, interned in the centers, are free.

From "The Story of My Life" by Michinobu Saga, approximately eighteen years old:

The plan for my future is very uncertain at present but I hope that after this crisis is over, life will be the same as pre-war. It is great to roam from place to place as I please without any person challenging my rights. Not only I, but the Japanese people as a group, hope that the relations between us and the white race will not be altered. We do not wish to bear anyone ill will and I know that the majority of the Americans do not hate us. I wanted to be a doctor, or be in a profession requiring some sort of science, but will most likely end up as a farmer. Because of the lack of opportunity, I must resign myself, at least until the war is over. I will not give up hope or faith.

Walking in Their Shoes

What would you do if you were released after several years of incarceration? Would you go back to where you came from? Go to a big city to find a job—maybe Chicago or New York? Try to go to college? What would it be like to find yourself in regular American society again? Would there be some things you'd miss about camp life, even as you embraced your freedom? Do you think your old friends would treat you any differently?

"My Future" by Herbert Yomogida

As the radio spokesman announced on the radio that the West Coast was being reopened, we couldn't believe it, but we listened tensely. My mother was fixing my sister's hair, my older sister was sweeping the floor while I was sitting near the stove when we heard this. We all at once crowded around the radio and listened. I could see our house which was built in 1939 with its venetian blinds, our lawn with the small magnolia tree standing in the center, my pals Dean Kirby and Louis Hoppis whom I used to play football with, our Presbyterian church on Locust Avenue, my new bunk bed, my junior high school and grammar school teachers, the bowling alley, the drugstores and the store on the corner of State Street, and all of the old familiar places. Most of all I want to go to the high school which was so big and modern, the football games and the pike on the beach. Yes, I really feel excited. But how do I know how our neighbors will treat me after I get back? I surely hope they will treat me like they did during the prewar days, but you have to expect a few of them to be prejudiced. I surely would want to see my schoolmates who would have really changed and are grown up, and our piano in the large living room with its large rug, radio and couches. Gee whiz, it doesn't really seem quite true, but it really is. I just can't wait to start playing football on the grass-covered lot with my old friends whom I really missed. I bet my mother just can't wait to go back to her new deluxe washing machine and her good old cooking.

But as we leave the relocation camps, I will be separated from many dear friends and teachers who have helped me enjoy my stay here. I surely will miss them.

My small sisters and baby brother who have practically grown up in camp will enjoy normally living. I surely am grateful for them and they will get ice creams and candies all the time. Yes, it will help make a happy future for us.

And one student penned an optimistic (and downright Dr. Seussian) poem about what lay before these students, should they be up to the challenge. "Goal Ahead"—written in English Period I at Rohwer, 1943:[11]

Those who "go places"
Know places to go,
Whether their pace is
Swift-footed or slow.
They are not haunted
By doubtings, but they
Travel, undaunted,
Their confident way.

Vim, vigor, vision
Brains, brilliance, and such,
Lacking decision
Won't get a man much.
Don't shilly-shally
But know what you're at.
Pick your own alley
And bowl 'em down that!

No one will wind up
Successfully, who
can't make his mind up
On what he would do;
Fix your selection
Of goals in your nut,
Go that direction
And nowhere else but!

1. David Robson, *The Internment of Japanese Americans* (San Diego, CA: ReferencePoint Press, 2014), 61–62.

2. Russell Bearden, "Japanese American Relocation Centers," Encyclopedia of Arkansas History & Culture, http://www.encyclopediaofarkansas.net/encyclopedia/entry-detail.aspx?entryID=2273.

3. *Rohwer Outpost*, March 10, 1943, Vol. II, no. 20, Record Group 1342, National Archives, quoted in Jan Fielder Ziegler, *The Schooling of Japanese American Children at Relocation Centers During World War II: Miss Mabel Jamison and Her Teaching of Art at Rohwer, Arkansas* (Lewiston, NY: The Mellen Press, 2005), 103.

4. Ziegler, *The Schooling of Japanese American Children*, 104.

5. Bearden, "Japanese American Relocation Centers."

6. War Relocation Authority, *The Evacuated People, A Quantitative Description*, 136–137, quoted in Russell Bearden, "Life Inside Arkansas's Japanese-American Relocation Centers." *Arkansas Historical Quarterly* 48 (Summer 1989): 192.

7. Quoted in Robson, *Internment*, 70.

8. Quoted in Robson, *Internment*, 71.

9. Robson, *Internment*, 73.

10. Autobiographies, Post Evacuation Plans, 1944; MSS 10-49, Box 5, folder 11. Rosalie Santine Gould–Mabel Jamison Vogel Collection, Butler Center for Arkansas Studies, Central Arkansas Library System, Little Rock, Arkansas.

11. Gould-Vogel Collection, Poetry, English Period I, Rohwer H.S., 1943; MSS 10-49, Box 5, folder 15.

Chapter 7
The Internment Experience Made Visual—Rohwer Camp Murals

Not only did the young people at Rohwer leave us their words in the form of diaries, autobiographies, and other writings, they also left us a visual representation of their experiences. Eight teenagers painted eight murals—which were captured in photographs, although the originals are now lost to history—depicting different aspects of internment, from the bombing of Pearl Harbor, to the arrival at assembly centers and Rohwer, to life in the camp, to plans for resettlement.

The journal of Mabel Jamison "Jamie" Vogel, art teacher at Rohwer, details the process by which the murals were created and explains each piece:

Rohwer Relocation Center, August 29, 1944: Murals

The history of evacuation as seen through the young eyes of eight high school students is recorded in murals adorning the interior of the new Rohwer auditorium. Done in poster tempera paint on beaver board, the murals measure 4 feet by 16 feet, and are displayed within eight panels just beneath the high windows—four on the east wall, and four on the west wall. They present a colorful and interesting spectacle against a background of white walls and brown stained wooded columns and trusses.

An evacuee representative of the Public Works Division approached the art class of the high school and requested the painting of the murals. Public Works was not particular what the subject matter might be. As long as the eight panel spaces were filled, the pictorial account could be of the Arkansas hill billy [sic], or of the Negroes [sic] so common in these parts. Since the time element was very limited, it was suggested that only four need be completed this year. The remaining four could be made next year. The matter was left entirely in the hands of the Art Department.

After a meeting of P.W. [Public Works] and Art Dept., it was decided that the "History of Evacuation" would be the most appropriate theme. In selecting the students to do the murals, those were sought who were the most talented, reliable, and who were sure of their stay in the Center throughout the period. Relocation [i.e., resettlement outside the camps] and segregation had been claiming students from time to time, and care was necessary so that it would not interrupt progress on the murals. It was agreed that all eight paintings would be done this year. To leave four to be done next year might mean that interest would lag into an anti-climax.

The Public Works Division offered to furnish all the painting material, the wall board, the lumber, for the construction of the large scaffolds. In turn, the Art Department promised to complete the paintings in time for the opening of the auditorium. The opening was scheduled for May 14, for the Senior Baccalaureate services in just eight weeks' time.

Work began immediately. The subject matter was condensed to eight main points: December 7th; Evacuation; Assembly Centers; To Rohwer; The New Home; Community Life; Center Occupations; and Relocation. Each student chose the topic of most interest to him.

The opportunity to participate in an activity of this nature is seldom offered to high school students. The favored students, therefore, showed much enthusiasm and interest, and the work took on intense earnestness. It was not easy, however. There was no pattern to follow. Each had to organize and develop his own ideas. The instructor's wish was that all the credit should go solely to the student; consequently, it was left up to each one to relate his own story in his own individual way.

[With all the work, the students] grew weary, and signs of strain were noticeable. As one student put it, "We were so happy and thrilled at the beginning, we all sang as we worked. But as the weeks passed, we got so tired of doing the same thing over and over, we were exhausted."

The last evening rolled around and the deadline had been met. There was cause for celebration this night, and all were in good spirits....Then six foremen of the Public Works Division surprised the students with refreshments of cold drinks and cakes. To climax the memorable evening, a photographer arrived about 11 p.m. and took pictures of each student posing beside his or her finished mural.

The following evening, at the Baccalaureate services, the public was given the opportunity to see the completed work of those eight high school students. Displayed to those who had experienced it, was the pictorial account of the evacuation and the ensuing events.

"December 7th" by Mas Kinoshita, 19 years old, grade 11A, is done in brilliant hues of reds and blues. Off to one side is a peaceful island sunset. The turning of a radio dial brings on the flash news and scenes of the bombing of Pearl Harbor.

"Evacuation" by Teruyo Kishi, 17, 10A, is a farewell to familiar scenes—the home, the fields, the public schools. There is dumping and burning of rubbish, and the selling of household items. In the background, an evacuation train is waiting to carry the people to some Assembly or evacuation center under military escort.

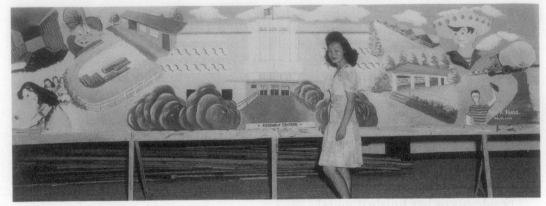

"Assembly Centers" by Mary Ihara, 17, 12A, features the main entrance to the Santa Anita racetrack grandstand. In the background is a horse stall which has been converted into sleeping quarters. There is a familiar scene from the Stockton Assembly Center—the old waterwagon sprinkling the dusty grounds and rows of barracks.

"To Rohwer" by Nobi Tanimoto, 20, 12B, pictures the train pulling into Rohwer with the evacuees—Rohwer, a place of cotton fields, of Negroes [*sic*] picking cotton, of swamps and cypress knees, of electrical storms—and then the black barracks which greet the eyes, with the guard tower in the foreground.

"The New Home" by Kik Toyofuku, 19 years, 12A, features the buildings of the center—the firehouse with the fire trucks; the hospital, its laundry and boiler-room, and the tall brick chimney; the auditorium; schools; mess halls and barracks; gardens and flowers.

"Community Life" by Michi Tanaka, 17, 12A, shows the various activities about camp—the flower arrangement classes, sports, weaving and dressmaking classes, Girl Reserves, the church, schools, adult talent shows, motion pictures, Toyland, and the dances.

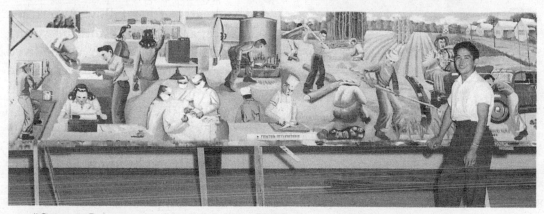

"Center Occupations" by Motchiko Hori, 18 years, 12A, relates the story of men and women at work on center jobs and projects. The carpenters, painters, boiler attendants, doctors, lumberjacks, farmers, tractor drivers, mess cooks and attendants.

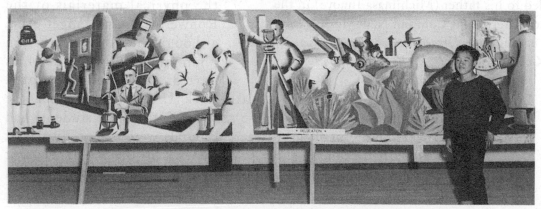

"Relocation" by Arthur Okusu, 17, 11A, shows the various professions and fields of endeavor on the "outside" which have encouraged the evacuees to resettle.

There is reflected in the paintings individuality of style and personality. [For instance, the] mural painted by the girl who had studied some dress designing shows her inclination toward drawing figures...

A good painting is a thing of lasting beauty. Long after the poster paint has peeled off the beaver boards, these murals, painted by these eight high school students will be remembered. For the story and history of the evacuation are not likely to be forgotten too soon. [1]

Historian Jan Ziegler wrote, "The murals were widely referenced in student and camp publications, and in Mrs. Jamison's personal correspondence during and after the camps' existence. Together with her students, and later, after the camps' closure, she displayed a specially prepared replica of the murals to interested groups in the community and beyond, working to dispel myths and fears, attempting to open minds and hearts of her fellow Americans regarding these unique young Americans who for a time lived among them."[2] Ziegler also noted that Jamison "clearly knew that through the filter of their art, these young people and the many others who would see the murals might know at a deeper level of comprehension what had happened, what was then happening, and what might happen in the future.[3]

The murals themselves, along with most of the rest of the physical materials of the Rohwer camp, no longer exist, although they are preserved in photographs. Also, in 2004, as part of the Life Interrupted

Not to be outdone by these older, more sophisticated muralists, a younger artist at Rohwer also weighed in on the internment experience, capturing the train, the barracks, and an American flag, as well as an airplane in a sunny sky. This drawing by first-grader Edward Inuoye was mailed to his father (Michimasa Inuoye) in the Lordsburg Internment Camp in New Mexico.
Courtesy of the Butler Center for Arkansas Studies, Rosalie Santine Gould–Mabel Jamison Vogel Collection

Project of the University of Arkansas at Little Rock (UALR) and the Japanese American National Museum (JANM), the sketch paintings the students had made on bed sheets before painting the actual murals were put on display at UALR. Jamie Vogel had donated these to the JANM in the 1980s. A grant from the Winthrop Rockefeller Foundation helped the JANM in its restoration efforts for these sketches. [4]

Notes
1. Rosalie Santine Gould–Mabel Jamison Vogel Collection. Butler Center for Arkansas Studies, Central Arkansas Library System, Little Rock, Arkansas. Text is

from Mabel Jamison Vogel's journal, "Murals" narrative, Rohwer Relocation Center, August 29, 1944. All the mural photos are from the Gould–Vogel Collection, except for "December 7th" by Mas Kinoshita, which is courtesy of the National Archives and Records Administration.

2. Jan Fielder Ziegler, *The Schooling of Japanese American Children at Relocation Centers During World War II: Miss Mabel Jamison and Her Teaching of Art at Rohwer, Arkansas* (Lewiston, NY: The Mellen Press, 2005), 71.

3. Jan Fielder Ziegler, "Listening to 'Miss Jamison': Lessons from the Schoolhouse at a Japanese Internment Camp, Rohwer Relocation Center," *Arkansas Review: A Journal of Delta Studies* 33 (August 2002): 143.

4. "Returning Beauty: Student Murals Back in Arkansas," *Arkansas Times*, October 7, 2004; Brian Niiya, Densho Encyclopedia, "Lasting Beauty: Miss Jamison and the Student Muralists (exhibition)."

The internees' time in Arkansas no doubt had a great impact on them, as well as on their children and their children's children and so on. Life was never the same again for these young people after the time they spent as government wards in the swamplands of Arkansas. The effects of relocation—financial, educational, personal, familial, spiritual—can never really be measured. After the camps closed in Arkansas—Jerome on June 30, 1944, and Rohwer on November 30, 1945—the Japanese Americans who had been in the state were scattered to the winds. Some returned to California, some moved to large non-coastal cities (at the U.S. government's encouragement) such as Chicago or St. Louis, some went to Hawaii or Japan. After being incarcerated by their government and with sentiments from the war lingering, they faced discrimination from the outside population as well as feelings of inadequacy and shame at having been imprisoned.

Will the Mistakes of the Past Be Repeated?

The September 11, 2001, attacks perpetrated by Muslims, men who professed to follow the religion of Islam, brought about discussion of how the country should act in regards to its Muslim population, echoing discussions about Japanese Americans following the bombing of Pearl Harbor. Some argued that Muslims in America should be put in camps, both to monitor their actions for any sign of terrorist plots and to protect them from possible harm from their fellow American citizens. This did not occur, although many Muslim Americans felt scrutinized and demonized following the 9/11 attacks.

Civil rights activist and former internee Fred Korematsu, who was at the heart of the landmark Supreme Court case *Korematsu v. United States* after he refused to leave his home in California in 1942, framed the discussion this way in a 2004 newspaper article: "I know what it is like to be at the other end of such scapegoating and how difficult it is to clear one's name after unjustified suspicions are endorsed as fact by the government. If someone is a spy or terrorist they should be prosecuted for their actions. But no one should ever be locked away simply because they share the same race, ethnicity, religion as a spy or terrorist. If that principle was not learned from the internment of Japanese Americans, then these are very dangerous times for our democracy." (Source: David Robson, *The Internment of Japanese Americans*, pp. 75–76)

Legacy for Japanese Americans

It is difficult to say what the true legacy of internment has been for Japanese Americans, particularly for those who were children and teenagers during their incarceration. It is impossible to know what their lives would have been like without the harrowing and transformative experience of having been imprisoned by their own government.

Many of those who were held in camps went on to successful careers and fulfilling lives. There is no doubt, however, that their education in particular was altered from what it would have been otherwise, affecting them forever. Long after the war, historian Lane Ryo Hirabayashi considered whether the assimilationist educational process, as well as the fact that "the war interrupted Nisei educational careers and, in some cases, terminated them forever,"

also may have "resulted in irreparable social and psychological consequences [for the students] that have never been fully acknowledged or accounted for."[1] He also compares the experience of the Japanese young people in the camps with "the experience of other racial-ethnic minorities—most notably a striking parallel with American Indian 'education' under the supervision of the Bureau of Indian Affairs. Education, from this point of view, is an actual instrument of assimilationist policy rather than an objective process designed to produce a populace that can think clearly and act upon its ideas and values."[2]

So, like the Native American children who were taken from their tribes to attend boarding schools in the late nineteenth and early twentieth centuries—to make them "more American"—these Japanese American young people were educated to act and speak in ways that were considered acceptable to American society, rather than preserving and finding pride in a unique ethnic heritage. It is also worth noting that the Native Americans were forcibly relocated from their tribal lands to what is now Oklahoma in the 1800s—another relocation by the U.S. government seen by most as less than noble. The effects of these actions, and the education imposed along with them, will linger forever.

Interestingly, just as people at the Jerome and Rohwer camps continued to identify themselves with what assembly center they went to, many of the internees maintained a strong identity with what camp they and/or

Liberty and Justice for All by Nancy Chikaraishi. Most children recited the pledge of allegiance in school, but the phrase "liberty and justice for all" is ironic, as these children and their families were detained in the internment camps—without liberty or justice. This painting was inspired by Chikaraishi's mother and father, who were held in the Rohwer camp when they first met. Ben Tsutomu Chikaraishi was twenty-one years old and Kiyo Chino was eighteen years old when they entered camp in 1942. They married on July 22, 1945, and resettled in Chicago after their time at Rohwer.
Courtesy of Nancy Chikaraishi and Ben Chikaraishi

their family members were held in, long after their release. The communities formed in the camps were communities of circumstance and imprisonment, but they were communities nonetheless. They became part of American history, but also family history for many.

Legacy for the Country

In the time since World War II, many historians have written about the incarceration experience, and institutions have begun collecting the history of the internment experience, as well as the greater Japanese American experience. Many who were held in the camps have given interviews and written memoirs. Many have also donated photos, letters, art, and other materials to institutions around the country that seek to preserve and interpret the history of Japanese internment.

For instance, the Japanese American National Museum—a Smithsonian Institution affiliate—opened in 1992 in the Little Tokyo area of Los Angeles, California, with the mission of promoting understanding and appreciation of America's ethnic and cultural diversity by sharing the Japanese American experience. The Manzanar Relocation Center in California, the best preserved of the camps, has been made a National Historic Landmark, under the control of the National Park Service. Photos, materials, and artwork from internees and their descendants can also be found around the country in various museum collections.

The experiences of the people who were interned or had family members who were interned continue to be reflected in artwork, books, and other forms of expression.

Legacy for the State of Arkansas

When Rohwer art teacher Jamie Vogel left Rohwer as the war came to an end, she took with her not only the friendship of former students, but also a commitment to continue her support of the Japanese American community, preserve the pieces of art her students had produced, and educate people about internment. After the war ended, Vogel corresponded with, and proved herself a lifeline to, many former camp residents. Particularly in the years immediately following the war, many in the Japanese American community experienced profound economic hardship. Through their former teacher, however, they were able to place their own art and creative pieces—jewelry, for example—into retail markets. Among those she helped was renowned Japanese American artist Henry Sugimoto.

Over the years, many people have returned to Arkansas to visit the place where they spent part of their childhood, or to see where their parents, grandparents, or great-grandparents once lived.

Actor George Takei, who lived at Rohwer as a boy, has returned to the state several times as part of various conferences and exhibits about internment.

Rohwer was added to the National Register of Historic Places on July 30, 1974. However, only a few concrete foundations and monuments—including a small cemetery and a monument to Japanese American soldiers who died

---

Henry Sugimoto, Artist of Internment

The artwork of noted artist Henry Sugimoto can be found in both the Smithsonian Institution in Washington DC and the Japanese American National Museum in LA. One painting also hangs at Hendrix College in Conway, Arkansas, where Sugimoto showed an exhibition of his work in 1944, while still interned. Sugimoto was held with his wife and daughter at the Jerome Relocation Center and then Rohwer after Jerome closed. Sugimoto served as art consultant to the War Relocation Authority, and he also taught art at Denson High School at Jerome during the 1943–44 school year.

This incarceration was a defining experience in Sugimoto's life. While interned, Sugimoto created about 100 paintings. For the rest of his career, Sugimoto continued to portray his memories of those three years. One of his most famous works is *When Can We Go Home?*, which portrays a Japanese mother and daughter surrounded by scenes of the relocation camp.

Leaving Arkansas in the summer of 1945, Sugimoto and his wife and daughter moved to New York City, where he lived for the rest of his life. From 1945 on, Sugimoto's paintings began to examine the relationship of Japanese immigrants to their adopted country and vice versa. While his time in the camps deeply affected him, it also strengthened his belief in the ideals upon which America was founded, and he became a naturalized citizen in 1952. He died in 1990.

(Source: Erin Branham, "Henry Yuzuro Sugimoto," Encyclopedia of Arkansas History & Culture)

fighting for America in World War II—remain. The WWII Japanese Internment Museum in McGehee, which opened in April 2013 in the renovated south building of the McGehee Railroad Depot, preserves materials from the Arkansas internment camps and features the *Against Their Will* exhibit about those interned at Jerome and Rohwer.

The ongoing Life Interrupted Project—a partnership between the University of Arkansas at Little Rock Public History program and the Japanese American National Museum in Los Angeles—seeks to amass an archive of documents and artifacts, raise money for conservation efforts at Jerome and Rohwer, make curriculum materials available to schools, and pursue further educational efforts by talking to groups, making presentations at academic conferences, and publishing

Jamie Vogel showing art created by Japanese Americans at Rohwer to students as part of her education efforts after internment had ended; circa 1950s.
Courtesy of the Butler Center for Arkansas Studies, Rosalie Santine Gould–Mabel Jamison Vogel Collection

research. The project held a conference in 2004 that attracted statewide, national, and international attention to the internment experience in Arkansas.

The Butler Center's Rosalie Santine Gould–Mabel Jamison Vogel Collection, donated in 2011, is housed in Little Rock in the Arkansas Studies Institute building and contains written works, photos, artwork, and other materials.

Rosalie Gould with a group of Japanese American visitors to Rohwer.
Courtesy of the Butler Center for Arkansas Studies, Rosalie Santine Gould–Mabel Jamison Vogel Collection

The Arkansas History Commission in Little Rock and other public and university archives in the state also hold papers and other materials from the Arkansas camps. People continue to donate materials to these institutions in hopes of preserving the history so others can learn about what they and their families experienced.

But there remains much to learn about this experience, from those who were there and from those who came after. And many voices are yet to be heard.

Rosalie Gould, mayor of McGehee, Arkansas, at the time, standing with the monuments at Rohwer; 1992. Rohwer art teacher Mabel Rose Jamison Vogel died in 1994 and willed her vast collection of Japanese American material to Gould, who became instrumental in preservation and education efforts related to Rohwer. She donated the collection to the Butler Center in 2011.
Courtesy of the Butler Center for Arkansas Studies, Rosalie Santine Gould–Mabel Jamison Vogel Collection

Notes

1. Lane Ryo Hirabayashi, "The Impact of Incarceration on the Education of Nisei Schoolchildren," in *Japanese Americans: From Relocation to Redress*, ed. Roger Daniels, Sandra C. Taylor, and Harry H. L. Kitano (Salt Lake City: University of Utah Press, 1986), 44.

2. Hirabayashi, "The Impact of Incarceration," 49.

George Takei Lives the Legacy of His Incarceration as a Child

George Takei, who gained international fame as Lieutenant Sulu in the original *Star Trek* television series and six movies, was held in the Rohwer camp for eight months when he was about five years old. His family then moved to the maximum-security camp at Tule Lake in California for the rest of the war following the refusal of Takei's parents to swear loyalty to the United States on the U.S. government's unfair loyalty questionnaire.

In his autobiography, *To the Stars*, he remembers how the word "Jap" has continued to affect him throughout his life. After the war, when his fourth-grade teacher referred to him as "that little Jap boy," he "felt shock, pain, rage, and shame all at the same time....But I found myself looking away... pretending I hadn't heard her. I just contained that terrible hot feeling inside. To this day, it angers me that I looked away. I didn't speak up. I swallowed my hurt.... Somehow, shame dominated my anger. I had the queasy feeling that her calling me 'Jap' had something to do with our having been in camp. And camp, I was old enough by now to know, was something like jail. It was a place where people who had done bad things were sent. I had a gnawing sense of guilt about our time spent in camp. I could not fully understand it, but I thought perhaps we had it coming to us to be punished like this. Maybe we deserved to be called this painful word, 'Jap.'...To a Japanese American, 'Jap' is a sound that vibrates with threat, an epithet sonorous with menace. Only a sound, an abbreviated word. Yet, the pain it can inflict and the injury it can cause lie in the force that history has hammered into it. 'Jap' has become more than a word. 'Jap' is an assault weapon.
(Source: George Takei, *To the Stars*, pp. 92–93)

Timeline of Events

1790

March 26: The U.S. Congress, in the Naturalization Act of March 26, 1790, states that "any alien, being a free white person who shall have resided within the limits and under the jurisdiction of the United States for a term of two years, may be admitted to become a citizen thereof."

1836

Arkansas becomes the 25th state. A state allowing slavery, it enters the Union with Michigan to maintain the balance between free and slave states.

1869

First group of Japanese immigrants arrives in the U.S. and establishes the Wakamatsu Colony at Gold Hill in California.

1873

The phrase "persons of African nativity or descent" is added to the language of the Naturalization Act of 1790, which is used to deny citizenship to Japanese and other Asian immigrants until 1952.

1882

May 6: Congress passes the Chinese Exclusion Act, which bars further Chinese immigration and prohibits Chinese from citizenship. Enforced from 1882 to 1892, it creates a labor demand, seen as the major reason for increased immigration of Japanese to the Pacific Coast.

Print by artist Hiroshige Andō (1797–1858) showing travelers at a rest stop near the harbor at Edo, Japan; 1856.

Courtesy of Library of Congress Prints and Photographs Division

1885

Japanese laborers begin arriving in Hawaii, recruited by plantation owners to work the sugarcane fields.

1891

Japanese immigrants arrive on the mainland U.S. for work primarily as agricultural laborers.

1894

June 27: A U.S. district court rules that Japanese immigrants cannot become citizens because they are not "free white people" as the act of 1790 requires.

1898

Hawaii is annexed by the U.S., enabling about 60,000 Japanese residing in Hawaii to proceed to the mainland U.S. without passports.

1900

The majority of Japanese immigrants come to the U.S. between 1900 and 1920. Under pressure from the U.S., the Japanese government eventually stops issuing passports to laborers desiring to enter the U.S. Since the territory of Hawaii is not mentioned in the agreement, Japanese continue to immigrate there.

May 7: The first large-scale anti-Japanese protest in California is held, organized by various labor groups.

1905

California urges the U.S. Congress to limit Japanese immigration.

May 14: Representatives from 67 organizations, including labor leaders and European immigrants, meet in San Francisco to form the Asiatic Exclusion League of San Francisco, marking the first organized effort of the anti-Japanese movement.

1906

October 11: San Francisco School Board orders segregation of 93 Japanese American students, as well as children of Chinese and Korean ancestry, from the majority population.

1907

As part of the informal Gentlemen's Agreement of 1907 between the U.S. and the Empire of Japan, Japan agrees not to issue passports for Japanese citizens wanting to work in the United States, thus effectively ending new Japanese immigration to America. In exchange, the United States agrees to accept the presence of Japanese immigrants already living in America, and to allow the immigration of Japanese workers' wives, children, and parents to America. As part of the agreement, President Theodore Roosevelt orders that the San Francisco School Board rescind the segregation order, but strong feelings against Japanese persist. Anti-Japanese riots break out in San Francisco in May, and again in October, much to the embarrassment of the U.S. government. Congress then passes an immigration bill forbidding Japanese laborers from entering the U.S. via Hawaii, Mexico, or Canada.

Japanese American man working in the lettuce fields in San Benito County, California, while he waits for evacuation orders; 1942.
Courtesy of Library of Congress Prints and Photographs Division

1913

The California Alien Land Law (Webb-Haney Act) passes, denying "all aliens ineligible for citizenship" (which includes all Asians except for Filipinos, who are "subjects" of the U.S.) the right to own land in California. Leasing land is limited to three years. Similar laws are eventually adopted in Washington, Oregon, Idaho, Montana, Arizona, New Mexico, Texas, Kansas, Louisiana, Missouri, Minnesota, Nebraska, Utah, Wyoming, and Arkansas.

1918

California's Alien Land Law is amended to close

loopholes. It forbids Issei (Japanese immigrants) to buy land in the names of their Nisei (American-born) children (see date 1913).

1920

A new, more stringent Alien Land Law passes as a ballot initiative in California, intending to close all loopholes found in the 1913 Alien Land Law.

Japanese American farmers produce $67 million worth of crops, more than ten percent of California's total crop value. There are 111,000 Japanese Americans in the U.S.—82,000 are immigrants and 29,000 were born in the U.S.

Arkansas's leading crop is cotton with over 40 percent of state farmland under cultivation producing the crop.

1922

November 13: Supreme Court rules in *Takeo Ozawa v. U.S.* that naturalization is limited to "free white persons and aliens of African nativity," thus legalizing the previous practice of excluding Asians from citizenship. This ban would last until 1952.

1924

Congress passes the Immigration Exclusion Act, barring all immigration from Japan to the U.S. Protests are held throughout Japan. July 1 is declared "Day of Humiliation."

1937

Japan invades China by the end of the year, capturing Nanking, capital of Nationalist China.

U.S. breaks off commercial relations with Japan.

1939

Britain and France declare war on Germany, which had invaded Poland, signaling beginning of World War II.

1941

August 14: In a letter to President Roosevelt, Representative John Dingell of

Crowned Queen of Cherry Blossoms; Washington DC, April 8, 1937. Sakiko Saito, daughter of the Japanese ambassador, was crowned Queen of the Cherry Blossoms by the commissioner of the District of Columbia as part of a festival celebrating the anniversary of the presentation of the Japanese cherry trees to the capital by the citizens of Tokyo, Japan.
Courtesy of Library of Congress Prints and Photographs Division

Protest in Washington DC to the president on the Japanese silk boycott; January 28, 1938. Following a protest parade to the White House, these members of the American Federation of Hosiery Workers presented an Anti-Boycott Memorial to President Franklin D. Roosevelt.
Courtesy of Library of Congress Prints and Photographs Division

Michigan suggests incarcerating 10,000 Hawaiian Japanese Americans as hostages to ensure "good behavior" on the part of Japan.

November 7: Report prepared by presidential investigator Curtis Munson and submitted to President Roosevelt, the State Department, and the Secretary of War certifies that Japanese Americans possess an extraordinary degree of loyalty to the U.S.—corroborated by years of surveillance by FBI and Naval Intelligence—and do not pose a threat to national security in the event of war with Japan.

A family tries to sell its belongings following the evacuation order for those of Japanese ancestry to leave areas of the West Coast; Los Angeles, California, 1942.
Courtesy of Library of Congress Prints and Photographs Division

November 12: Fifteen Japanese American businessmen and community leaders in Los Angeles's Little Tokyo are picked up in an FBI raid. Records and membership lists for such organizations as the Japanese Chamber of Commerce and the Central Japanese Association are seized. The fifteen men cooperate with authorities, while a spokesman for the Central Japanese Association makes this statement: "We teach the fundamental principles of America and the high ideals of American democracy. We want to live here in peace and harmony. Our people are 100% loyal to America."

December 7: Japan bombs U.S. fleet and military base at Pearl Harbor in Hawaii. Over U.S. 3,500 servicemen are wounded or killed. Martial law is declared in Hawaii.

December 7: The FBI begins arresting Japanese immigrants identified as community leaders: priests, Japanese language teachers, newspaper publishers, and heads of organizations. Within 48 hours, 1,291 are arrested. Most of these men would be incarcerated for the duration of the war, separated from their families.

December 8: U.S. Congress declares war on Japan. Within hours, the FBI arrests 736 Japanese resident aliens deemed security risks in Hawaii and on the mainland U.S.

Evacuees from California waiting with their luggage for a train; April 1942.
Courtesy of Library of Congress Prints and Photographs Division

December 11: The Western Defense Command is established with Lt. Gen. John L. DeWitt as the commander.

December 1941–January 1942: The FBI searches thousands of Japanese American homes on the West Coast for contraband. Short-wave radios, cameras, heirloom swords, and explosives used for clearing stumps in agriculture are among the items confiscated. Over 2,000 Issei in Hawaii and on the mainland—teachers, priests, officers of organizations, newspaper editors, and

other prominent people in the Japanese community—are imprisoned by the
U.S. government.

1942

Confusion and rumors of subversion abound. U.S. and Allied forces suffer catastrophic defeats for four months, heightening the threat of a West Coast invasion by Japan.

January 5: War Department classifies Japanese American men of draft age 4-C "enemy aliens." Status not changed until June 16, 1946.

February 19: President Roosevelt signs Executive Order 9066, giving the Secretary of War authority to designate "military areas from which to exclude certain people." The order did not specify Japanese Americans, but they were the only group to be imprisoned on a mass scale as a result of it. Eventually 120,000 Japanese—aliens and citizens—will be relocated.

February 27: Idaho governor Chase Clark tells a congressional committee in Seattle that Japanese would be welcome in Idaho only if they were in "concentration camps under military guard." Some credit Clark with the conception of what was to come.

Japanese American child who will go with her parents to an assembly center; Los Angeles, California, April 1942. *Courtesy of Library of Congress Prints and Photographs Division*

March 2: Public Proclamation #1 issued by Lt. General John L. DeWitt, head of the Western Defense Command, specifies military zones 1 and 2. Zone 1 includes western halves of California, Washington, and Oregon and the southern third of Arizona. A curfew goes into effect; all those of Japanese ancestry must remain at home from 8 p.m. to 6 a.m.

March 18: The president signs Executive Order 9102 establishing the War Relocation Authority (WRA) with Milton Eisenhower (younger brother of U.S. president Dwight D. Eisenhower) as director.

March: The Wartime Civil Control Administration opens 16 Assembly Centers, 13 of which are in California, to detain approximately 92,000 men, women, and children until the permanent incarceration camps are completed. Most of the California residents who eventually end up in Arkansas are assigned to the Santa Anita center (operating March 27 through October 27, 1942) or the Stockton center (operating May 10 through October 17, 1942).

Japanese American child who will go with his parents to an assembly center; Los Angeles, California, April 1942. *Courtesy of Library of Congress Prints and Photographs Division*

May: The evacuees begin transfer to permanent WRA incarceration facilities or "camps." They total ten: Manzanar, Poston, Gila River, Topaz, Granada, Heart

June 5: Incarceration of people of Japanese ancestry from designated military zones is now complete.

A general view of quarters for evacuees of Japanese ancestry who will be transferred later to War Relocation Authority centers for the duration of the war; Santa Anita Assembly Center, Arcadia, California, April 1942.
Courtesy of Library of Congress Prints and Photographs Division

June 17: Milton Eisenhower resigns as WRA director. Dillon Myer is appointed to replace him.

July 1: Construction begins on Rohwer Relocation Center by the Linebarger-Senne Construction Company of Little Rock, Arkansas.

July 15: Construction begins on Jerome Relocation Center by A. J. Rife Construction Company of Dallas, Texas.

August 4: A routine search for contraband at the Santa Anita assembly center turns into something of a riot. Eager military personnel had become overzealous and abusive, which, along with the failure of several attempts to reach the camp's internal security chief, triggers mass unrest, crowd formation, and the harassing of the searchers. Military police with tanks and machine guns quickly end the incident. The overzealous military personnel are later replaced.

September: Inmates of assembly centers begin the transfer to the more permanent camps.

September 18: The first inmates arrive at Rohwer, Arkansas, from California after a three-day train ride from the assembly centers to reach Arkansas.

Japanese Americans waiting to be registered at the Santa Anita Assembly Center; Los Angeles, California, April 1942.
Courtesy of Library of Congress Prints and Photographs Division

Background: The Rohwer Relocation Center is constructed in 1942 on approximately 10,161 acres in Desha County southeastern Arkansas. The site is located about 110 miles southeast of Little Rock and about 27 miles north of the Jerome Relocation Center. Approximately 500 acres serve as the central area of the relocation center and are home to most of the structures. There are more than 620 buildings at the center including buildings for housing, military police, staff, fire station, health care, and mess halls.

Evacuees working outside the fenced area are subject to harassment caused by mistaken identity. Early in the relocation center occupation, evacuee volunteers clearing brush are reportedly taken off to a local jail at gunpoint by local residents who thought they were Japanese paratroopers.

October 6: Camp at Jerome, Arkansas, opens. Evacuees are from California and Hawaii.

Background: The Jerome Relocation Center is constructed in 1942 on approximately 500 acres in Drew and Chicot counties in southeastern Arkansas. The site is located about 120 miles southeast of Little Rock and about 27 miles south of the Rohwer Relocation Center. The relocation center is in operation from October 6, 1942, until June 30, 1944. The center is the last internment camp to open and the first to close. There are more than 610 buildings at the relocation center, including buildings for barracks, military police, staff, fire station, health care, and mess halls. After the relocation center closes, it is converted into a prisoner-of-war camp for Germans.

Evacuees boarding a train at the Santa Anita Assembly Center in California en route to a War Relocation Center; 1942.
Courtesy of Library of Congress Prints and Photographs Division

November 17: A tenant farmer on horseback on his way home from deer hunting comes across three Japanese Americans at Jerome on a work detail in the woods. Thinking the Japanese Americans are trying to escape, he fires one round of buckshot, wounding two of them. Referring to the presence of a white engineer supervisor, the farmer explains that he thought the supervisor was trying to aid the escape.

1943

Early 1943: Jerome reaches its maximum population of 8,497, and Rohwer reaches its maximum population of 8,475.

January 28: War Department announces plans to organize an all–Japanese American combat unit and calls for volunteers in Hawaii (where Japanese Americans were under the authority of the U.S. Army but generally not relocated) and from among men in the camps.

January 29: A War Department press release announces the registration program for both recruitment and leave clearance.

February 8: Loyalty questionnaire administered in all ten camps to men and women over the age of seventeen. Contradictory and confusing nature of questions causes conflicts in families.

March: Approximately 10,000 Japanese American men volunteer for the armed services from Hawaii. About 1,200 volunteer out of the camps.

April: 442nd Regimental Combat Team is activated.

April 13: "A Jap's a Jap. There is no way to determine their loyalty....This coast is too vulnerable. No Jap should come back to this coast except on a permit from my office," General John L. DeWitt, head of the Western Defense Command, states before the House Naval Affairs Subcommittee.

July – November 1944: Jerome produces over 280,000 board feet of lumber and over 6,000 cords of firewood (from inmates clearing trees). In 1943, 630 acres are put under cultivation at Jerome. In 1944, 718 acres are under cultivation, 200 additional acres are cleared but not farmed, and several hundred more acres are partially cleared.

1944

January 20: The draft is reinstated for Japanese Americans, including those in the camps. The vast majority comply, but a few hundred resist and are brought up on federal charges. Most of the resisters are imprisoned in a federal penitentiary.

Rohwer Monument to the 100th Battalion and 442nd Regimental Combat Team; April 1992. The Rohwer National Historic Landmark contains several monuments made by inmates during their internment, including one that honors Japanese Americans who died fighting for America in World War II.
Courtesy of the Butler Center for Arkansas Studies, Rosalie Santine Gould–Mabel Jamison Vogel Collection

June 30: Jerome becomes the first camp to close, with the last inmates being transferred to Rohwer and other camps.

The closure of the Jerome Relocation Center is cited as a sign of the WRA's success in placing Japanese Americans in jobs and homes outside of the West Coast restricted zone. The overall population of the ten relocation centers declined in 1944 as over 18,000 evacuees moved out through the WRA leave and resettlement process. Jerome was chosen for closure for three reasons: it was the least developed of the relocation centers, it had one of the smallest populations remaining in the camp, and the nearby Rohwer Relocation Center could absorb most of the Jerome residents, reducing the amount of transportation needed.

October 30: The forces of the 100th Battalion and 442nd Regimental Combat

Team—composed almost entirely of Japanese Americans—rescue the Texas "lost battalion" in France after five days of battle. The battle results in 800 casualties, including 184 killed in action, to rescue the 211 Texans. After this rescue, the Japanese American soldiers are ordered to keep advancing in the forest; they would push ahead without relief or rest until November 9. According to the Densho Encyclopedia, the rescue raised the question of whether the Nisei soldiers were seen as "cannon fodder" or whether their outstanding performance led to their being given the most difficult assignments.

October: Residents of Rohwer erect monuments in the camp cemetery. One monument, in the shape of a military tank, is to the Japanese Americans in the 100th Battalion and the 442nd Regimental Combat Team who were killed in Italy and France. Another is to those who died in the relocation center. It has both Japanese and English inscriptions. The Japanese translates to: "May the people of Arkansas keep in beauty and reverence forever this ground where our bodies sleep." The English inscription reads: "Erected by the inhabitants of Rohwer Relocation Center October 1944."

December 17: Public Proclamation No. 21 is issued, revoking the West Coast exclusion order against Japanese Americans (effective on January 2, 1945, in anticipation of possible negative ruling of Supreme Court the following day).

December 18: U.S. Supreme Court rules that detention orders are a valid use of "war powers" in the *Korematsu* case. In the *Endo* case, it declares that the WRA cannot detain loyal citizens against their will, paving the way for Japanese Americans to return to the West Coast. The Court announced its decision on both cases on December 18, but the day before the Supreme Court decisions were announced, the War Department preempted the verdicts with a press release stating that it was revoking the mass incarceration order.

Photograph showing atomic bomb mushroom cloud over Nagasaki, Japan; August 9, 1945. *Courtesy of Library of Congress Prints and Photographs Division*

1945

January 2: Restrictions preventing resettlement on the West Coast are removed, although many exceptions continue to exist. A few carefully screened Japanese Americans had returned to the coast in late 1944.

August 6: U.S. drops atomic bomb on Hiroshima, Japan, killing or wounding at least 150,000 people, mostly civilians.

August 9: U.S. drops atomic bomb on Nagasaki, Japan, killing or wounding at least 75,000 people.

After the bombings, at least three million Japanese are left homeless. The cities' citizens also face long-term health consequences from radiation sickness, illness, and malnutrition.

September 2: Japan formally surrenders.

September 4: Western Defense Command issues Public Proclamation No. 24, revoking all West Coast exclusion orders against those of Japanese ancestry. Some 44,000 people still remain in the camps. Many have nowhere to go, having lost their homes and jobs. Many are afraid of anti-Japanese hostility and refuse to leave.

November 30: Rohwer, Arkansas, camp closes. After the relocation center was closed, 120 acres were deeded to the local school district and the remaining land was sold back to the original farmers or to veterans. Equipment and buildings were sold to bidders from across the country.

1946

March 20: The Tule Lake "segregation center," the last of the ten major concentration camps, closes, in what was termed "a mass evacuation in reverse." In the month prior to the closing, some 5,000 internees had had to be moved, many of whom were elderly, impoverished, or mentally ill and with no place to go. Of the 554 people left there at the beginning of the day, 450 are moved to the Crystal City detention facility in Texas (run by the Immigration and Naturalization Service), 60 are released, and the rest are relocated elsewhere.

July 15: As he receives the 442nd Regimental Combat Team on the White House Lawn, President Harry Truman says, "You not only fought the enemy but you fought prejudice...and you won."

1947

December 12: President Truman grants pardons to all 267 Japanese American draft resisters.

1948

January 19: U.S. Supreme Court invalidates the California Alien Land Law, which denied gift of land by immigrant Japanese to citizen children.

July 12: President Truman signs "Evacuation Claims Act," which would pay less than ten cents on the dollar for lost property only. Although approximately $28 million was paid from this act, this was only a small fraction of the estimated loss in income and property. Many former internees cannot produce required documentary proof of losses.

1952

April 17: California Supreme Court declares racially restrictive alien land laws unenforceable.

June 27: Walter-McCarran Immigration and Nationality Act passes in Congress over President Truman's veto. Truman considers the act too restrictive in its quota system, which heavily favors northern European nations. However, the act allows Japanese and other Asian immigrants to become naturalized citizens for the first time.

1954

The Supreme Court rules in *Brown v. Board of Education of Topeka* and requires segregated public schools to be integrated.

1955

Orval E. Faubus is elected to his first two-year term as Arkansas's governor. He will serve a total of six terms, from 1955 to 1967.

1957

President Eisenhower sends U.S. troops to help nine African American high school students attend Central High School in Little Rock. He also federalizes the Arkansas National Guard, which had previously been ordered by Governor Faubus to prevent the students from entering. Eisenhower's actions upheld the Supreme Court's *Brown v. Board of Education* decision and became one of the first steps in the American civil rights movement.

Rohwer cemetery sign that was relocated to the WWII Japanese American Internment Museum at McGehee in 2014. The sign's arrow points in the direction of Rohwer.
Photo by Sarah Raycher

1959

August 29: Hawaii becomes the fiftieth U.S. state. Daniel Inouye is the first Japanese American elected to the House of Representatives.

1970

July 10: A resolution by the JACL's Northern California-Western Nevada District Council calling for reparations for the World War II incarceration of Japanese Americans is announced. Titled "A Requital Supplication" and championed by Edison Uno, this resolution would have the JACL seek a bill in Congress awarding individual compensation on a per diem basis, tax-free.

1974

July 30: The remains of the Rohwer site in Arkansas are added to the National Register of Historic Places.

1976

President Gerald Ford signs proclamation titled "An American Promise" rescinding Executive Order 9066.

1979

November 28: Representative Mike Lowry (D-Wash.) introduces the World War II Japanese-American Human Rights Violations Act (H.R. 5977) into Congress. It proposes direct payments of $15,000 per victim plus an additional $15 per day interned.

1980

July 31: President Jimmy Carter signs a bill to create the Commission on Wartime Relocation and Internment of Civilians (CWRIC) to determine whether any wrongs had been committed in the internment of 120,000 Japanese Americans, and also of 1,000 Aleutian and Pribilof Islanders. CWRIC is to recommend remedies.

1981

CWRIC holds hearings in nine major cities from July 14 through December 9 as part of its investigation into the internment of Japanese Americans during World War II. The emotional testimony by Japanese American witnesses about their wartime experiences would prove cathartic for the community and might be considered a turning point in the redress movement. In all, some 750 witnesses testify.

1983

June: CWRIC issues its report, *Personal Justice Denied*, concluding that the exclusion, expulsion, and incarceration of Japanese Americans was not justified by "military necessity," and that the decision was based on "race prejudice, war hysteria and a failure of political leadership." It recommends that Congress pass legislation that recognizes "grave injustice" done, offers the nation's apologies, and gives $20,000 in compensation to each of the estimated 60,000 survivors.

1984

The California State Legislature proclaims on February 19, 1984, that February 19 of each year will be recognized as "A Day of Remembrance" of the concentration episode to encourage Californians to reflect upon their shared responsibility to uphold the Constitution and the rights of all individuals at all times.

1987

September 17: Congress passes the Civil Liberties Act.

1988

April 20: Senate passage of Civil Liberties Act of 1988.

August 10: President Ronald Reagan signs Civil Liberties Act of 1988, requiring payment of $20,000, an apology to the estimated 60,000 survivors of internment, and a $1.25 billion education fund.

1989

November 21: President George H. W. Bush signs appropriation bill, containing a redress payment provision under the entitlement program.

1990

October 9: First letters of apology signed by President Bush are presented to oldest survivors of internment at a Department of Justice ceremony along with redress payment of $20,000. The 107-year-old Rev. Mamoru Eto of Los Angeles is the first to receive his check.

1992

Arkansas governor Bill Clinton is elected the 42nd president of the United States. As president, in 1999, he signs the last letters of apology sent to Japanese Americans with their redress.

The Japanese American National Museum opens in Los Angeles, California.

1996

President Clinton appoints the commissioners to the Civil Liberties Public Education Fund (CLPEF).

1999

February 5: The Office of Redress Administration officially closes its doors, having distributed redress payments of more than $1.6 billion to 82,250 claimants.

Internment museum in McGehee, Arkansas; 2015.
Photo by Sarah Raycher

June 5: The Go for Broke Monument is dedicated in Los Angeles to honor segregated Japanese American units: the 100th Infantry Battalion, 442nd Regimental Combat Team, MIS (Military Intelligence Service), 522nd Field Artillery Battalion, 232nd Combat Engineer Company, 1399th Engineering Construction Battalion, and the many other men and women who served overseas during World War II. It is engraved with the names of more than 16,000 Nisei who fought in the war.

2000

November 9: In a memo to Secretary of the Interior Bruce Babbitt, President Clinton requests that the Department of the Interior make recommendations to preserve the World War II Japanese American interment sites. Clinton states, "The Japanese American internment sites represent a tangible reminder of the grave injustice done to Japanese Americans."

That same day, the Japanese American Memorial to Patriotism During World War II—a National Park Service site—is dedicated in Washington DC.

2001

January 9: Secretary of the Interior Bruce Babbitt delivers the "Report to the President: Japanese American Internment Sites Preservation."

2004

The University of Arkansas at Little Rock hosts a conference as part of its Life Interrupted Project that attracts statewide, national, and international attention to the internment experience in Arkansas.

2011

Rosalie Gould of McGehee, Arkansas, donates her collection of materials to the Butler Center for Arkansas Studies in Little Rock. The collection—

containing school-related materials from the Rohwer Relocation Center, including autobiographies of Japanese American students interned at Rohwer, correspondence, clippings, pamphlets, photographs, and various other items—had been preserved by Rohwer art teacher Mabel Rose Jamison Vogel and given to Gould upon Vogel's death. Both women had worked for years in educating people about the Japanese internment experience, especially at the Arkansas camps. As Butler Center manager David Stricklin said at the time of the donation, the Rosalie Santine Gould–Mabel Jamison Vogel Collection is a testament to "Mrs. Gould's determination to help preserve the history of the [Rohwer] camp, her friendship with Mrs. Vogel, her decision to keep the collection together in the many years since Mrs. Vogel's death, and the relationships she has formed with people all over the world who are interested in the collection. These include people who lived at the camp, their kids, art historians, and other scholars." The donation sparks educational outreach and other ongoing projects at the Butler Center, including the art exhibition *The Art of Living* in fall 2011, which was made possible by a grant from the National Park Service.

2013

The WWII Japanese Internment Museum opens in McGehee in a renovated building of the McGehee Railroad Depot. The museum preserves materials from the Arkansas internment camps and features the *Against Their Will* exhibit about those interned at Jerome and Rohwer.

2015

The UALR Center for Arkansas History and Culture announces the launch of *Rohwer Restored*, a virtual exhibit that documents a project to stabilize and restore the Rohwer Japanese American Relocation Center Cemetery. Funded in part by the National Park Service's Japanese American Confinement Sites Grant Program, the project seeks to restore the headstones, flower holders, pathways, and monuments at Rohwer. More information can be found at ualrexhibits.org/rohwer/.

Source: Timeline adapted from the Life Interrupted Project, a partnership between the University of Arkansas at Little Rock and the Japanese American National Museum in Los Angeles, California. Online at http://www.ualr.edu/lifeinterrupted/.

Internet Resources:

The Art of Living: Japanese American Creative Experience at Rohwer. Butler Center for Arkansas Studies, Central Arkansas Library System. http://www.butlercenter.org/rohwer/index.html

Children of the Camps. http://www.pbs.org/childofcamp/index.html

Densho Encyclopedia Digital Archive. www.densho.org/archive/

Encyclopedia of Arkansas History & Culture. www.encyclopediaofarkansas.net

Japanese American National Museum. www.janm.org/collections/

Life Interrupted Project. University of Arkansas at Little Rock. http://www.ualr.edu/lifeinterrupted/

National Park Service, Department of the Interior. Rohwer Relocation Center Memorial Cemetery, Rohwer, Arkansas. http://www.nps.gov/nr/travel/Asian_American_and_Pacific_Islander_Heritage/Rohwer-Relocation-Center-Memorial-Cemetery.htm

Online Center for the Study of Japanese American Concentration Camp Art. www.lib.iastate.edu/internart-main/6786

Rohwer Heritage Site. Arkansas State University. http://rohwer.astate.edu/

Smithsonian: National Museum of American History. http://americanhistory.si.edu/perfectunion/experience/index.html

Young Adult Fiction/Memoir:

Denenberg, Barry. *The Journal of Ben Uchida: Citizen 13559 Mirror Lake Internment Camp* (My Name is America series). New York: Scholastic Inc., 2003. *Fictionalized journal of a twelve-year-old boy held in one of America's Japanese internment camps during World War II.*

Morrill, Jan. *The Red Kimono.* Fayetteville: University of Arkansas Press, 2013. *Historical fiction from the perspective of nine-year-old Sachiko Kumura and her seventeen-year-old brother Nobu, who are forced to leave California to be interned in Arkansas, as well as teenager Terrence Harris, whose act of violence after the bombing of Pearl Harbor leads to his incarceration as well.*

Schiffer, Vivienne. *Camp Nine.* Fayetteville: University of Arkansas Press, 2013. *The story of how a young girl's childhood was transformed by the appearance of Japanese Americans who were interned at "Camp Nine," a fictionalized version of the Rohwer Relocation Center.*

Wakatsuki, Jeanne Houston, and James D. Houston. *Farewell to Manzanar*. New York: Houghton Mifflin Company, 1973, 2002. *Memoir in which thirty-seven-year-old Jeanne Wakatsuki looks back at her time spent at the Manzanar internment camp when she was a child.*

Books and Articles:

Anderson, William G. "Early Reaction in Arkansas to the Relocation of Japanese in the State." *Arkansas Historical Quarterly* 23 (Autumn 1964): 196–211.

Bearden, Russell E. "The False Rumor of Tuesday: Arkansas's Internment of Japanese-Americans." *Arkansas Historical Quarterly* 41 (Winter 1982): 327–339.

———. "Life Inside Arkansas's Japanese-American Relocation Centers." *Arkansas Historical Quarterly* 47 (Summer 1989): 170–196.

Daniels, Roger. *Concentration Camps: North America*. Malabar, FL: Robert E. Krieger Publishing Co. Inc., 1981.

Hirasuna, Delphine. *The Art of Gaman: Arts and Crafts from the Japanese American Internment Camps, 1942–1946*. Berkeley, CA: Ten Speed Press, 2005.

Howard, John. *Concentration Camps on the Home Front: Japanese Americans in the House of Jim Crow*. Chicago: University of Chicago Press, 2008.

Inada, Lawson Fusao, ed. *Only What We Could Carry: The Japanese Internment Experience*. Berkeley, CA: Heyday Books, 2000.

Irons, Peter, ed. *Justice Delayed: The Record of the Japanese American Internment Cases*. Middletown, CT: Wesleyan University Press, 1989.

Kashima, Tetsuden. *Judgment without Trial: Japanese American Imprisonment during World War II*. Seattle: University of Washington Press, 2003.

Kim, Kristine. *Henry Sugimoto: Painting an American Experience*. Berkeley, CA: Heyday Books, 2000.

Murray, Alice Yang. *Historical Memories of the Japanese American Internment and the Struggle for Redress*. Stanford, CA: Stanford University Press, 2008.

Ng, Wendy L. *Japanese American Internment during World War II: A History and Reference Guide*. Westport, CT: Greenwood Press, 2002.

Robson, David. *The Internment of Japanese Americans*. San Diego, CA: ReferencePoint Press, Inc., 2014.

Smith, C. Calvin. "The Response of Arkansas to Prisoners of War and Japanese Americans in Arkansas, 1942–1945." *Arkansas Historical Quarterly* 53 (Autumn 1994): 340–364.

———. *War and Wartime Changes: The Transformation of Arkansas, 1940–1945*. Fayetteville: University of Arkansas Press, 1986.

Takei, George. *To the Stars: The Autobiography of George Takei, Star Trek's Mr. Sulu.* New York: Simon & Schuster, 1994.

Tateishi, John. *And Justice for All: An Oral History of the Japanese American Detention Camps.* Seattle and London: University of Washington Press, 1984.

Twyford, Holly Feltman. "Nisci in Arkansas: The Plight of Japanese American Youths in the Arkansas Internment Camps of World War II." MA thesis, University of Arkansas, 1993.

Ward, Jason Morgan. "'No Jap Crow': Japanese Americans Encounter the World War II South." *Journal of Southern History* 73 (February 2007). 75–104.

Wu, Hui. "Writing and Teaching behind Barbed Wire: An Exiled Composition Class in a Japanese-American Internment Camp." *College Composition and Communication* 59, no. 2 (December 2007): 237–262.

Yenne, Bill. *Rising Sons: The Japanese American GIs Who Fought for the United States in World War II.* New York: Thomas Dunne Books, 2007.

Ziegler, Jan Fielder. "Listening to 'Miss Jamison': Lessons from the Schoolhouse at a Japanese Internment Camp, Rohwer Relocation Center." *Arkansas Review: A Journal of Delta Studies* 33 (August 2002): 137–146.

———. *The Schooling of Japanese American Children at Relocation Centers During World War II: Miss Mabel Jamison and Her Teaching of Art at Rohwer, Arkansas.* Lewiston, NY: The Mellen Press, 2005.

Questions:

❏ Do you think, based on the fear at the time that Japanese Americans might help Japan in the war against the United States, that internment was justified? Why or why not?

❏ How do you think the experience of internment differed for the younger generation versus the older generation? What long-term effects do you think it had on individuals and families?

❏ If you had to leave your home and go to a camp across the country, what would you bring? Pick five items that are absolutely essential to you. What would you bring if you knew you would not have access to electricity?

❏ Do you think we have made any strides in how we deal with ethnic and other kinds of diversity in America?

❏ If someone read about you and your experiences seventy years later, what would you want them to know about you?

Exercises:

Walking in Their Shoes

Put yourself in the shoes of the young people held in the Arkansas camps and imagine you are a Japanese American teenager during World War II.

❏ How would you artistically represent your experience of internment? Draw a mural showing the experience of leaving home or living in an internment camp.

❏ Using a limited amount of raw materials—such as rocks, shells, and paint—create something that either says something about being displaced or captures something about yourself.

❏ Write a letter as if you are writing to a friend you left behind. What would you ask about what was going on back home? What would you say about your experience? Would you be completely honest about how you felt?

See also *Walking in Their Shoes* segments throughout the book, pp. 11, 35, 43, 58, 63, 70, 85.

Walking in Your Own Shoes

❏ People become displaced in America and around the world for many reasons: war, drought, floods, famine. For instance, people came to Arkansas from Louisiana or Mississippi following Hurricane Katrina in 2005. Families also separate and move for other reasons, too, such as divorce or a new job. Consider what you would do if you had to leave home to go someplace new—or reflect on the experience if you have ever been displaced from your home.

❏ Write a diary entry for the day you leave home and for the day you arrive at your new home.

❏ Record a "day in the life" at your new home, hour by hour.

❏ Write a poem, short story, or song that captures how you feel.

About the Editor

Ali Welky started her editorial career working for the children's book publisher Scholastic Inc. She is currently the assistant editor of the online *Encyclopedia of Arkansas History & Culture*, a project of the Butler Center for Arkansas Studies at the Central Arkansas Library System in Little Rock. She holds a BA in English from Truman State University in Kirksville, Missouri, and an MA in English from the University of Central Arkansas in Conway. She co-edited the *Encyclopedia of Arkansas Music* (Butler Center Books, 2013). She lives in Conway with her husband and two children.

Photo by Mike Keckhaver

CPSIA information can be obtained
at www.ICGtesting.com
Printed in the USA
LVOW02s1016150116

470252LV00002B/2/P